The Beale Road

Written and Compiled

By

L. J. Martin

Edward Fitzgerald Beale

The Camel Expedition

Published by

2

Buttonwillow Books

48 Rock Creek Road

Clinton, Montana 59825

buttonwillowbooks@gmail.com

Copyright 2021 L. J. Martin

ISBN: 9798597555317

Fort Leavenworth
Council Grove
Fort Smith
San Antonio
TEXAS
TEXAS
TERRITORY OF KANSAS
UNORGANIZED TERRITORY
Santa Fe Trail
BENT'S FORT
Wagon Road Expedition, 1858–59
Fort Clark
Fort Lancaster
Fort Davis
RATON PASS
Taos Trail
TAOS
SANTA FE
Camel Expedition, 1857–58
Rio Grande
El Paso del Norte
SOCORRO
ALBUQUERQUE
Gila Trail
Old Spanish Trail
TERRITORY OF UTAH
Fort Defiance
TERRITORY OF NEW MEXICO
Gila River
Tucson
Colorado River
Las Vegas
Beale's Crossing
SAN DIEGO
FORT YUMA
FORT TEJON
CALIFORNIA
MONTEREY
SAN FRANCISCO

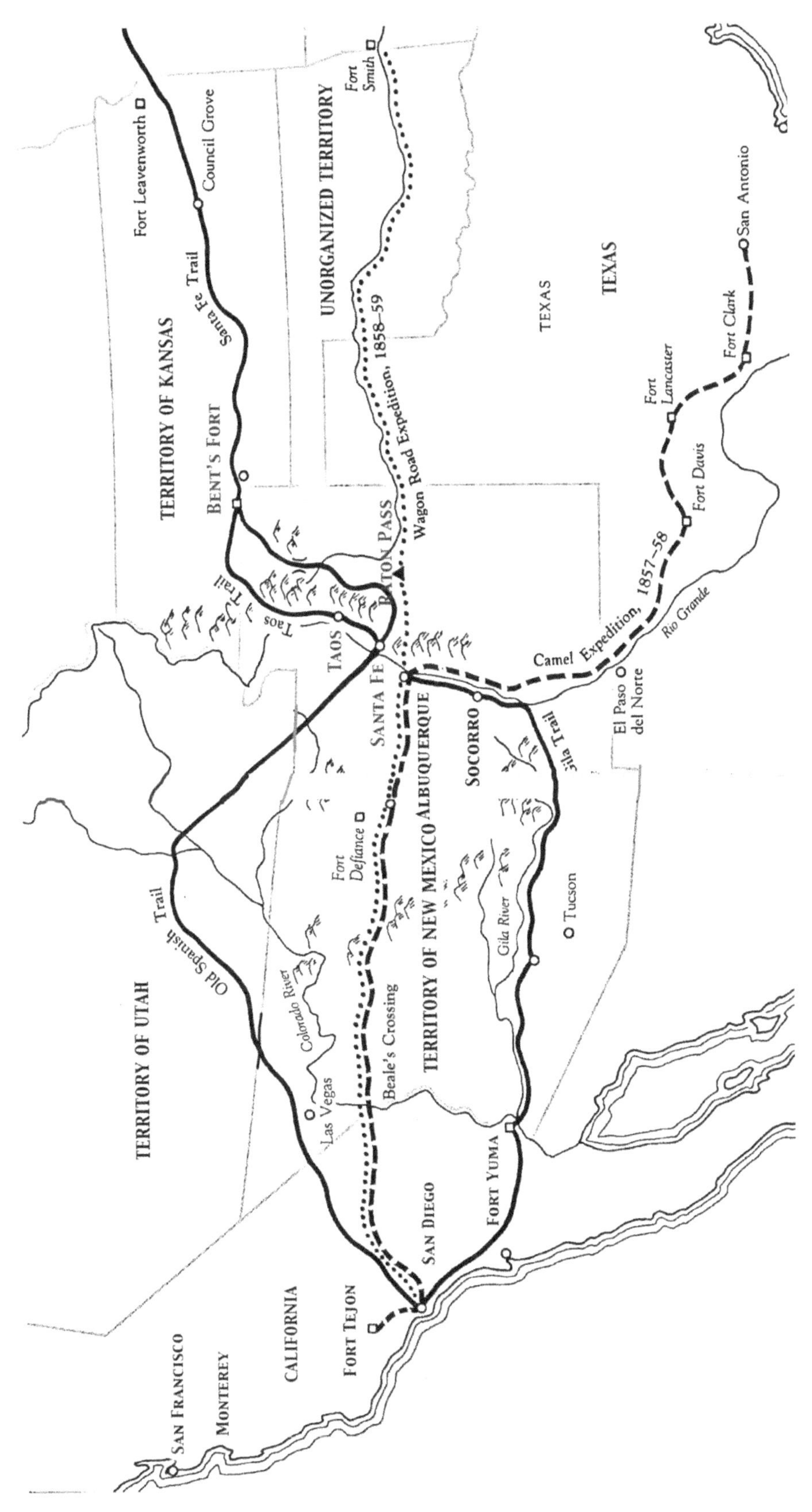

3

The pages of Beale's report to Congress have been scanned from the actual document so some are slightly tweaked and a little difficult to read, however you know you're getting the report word-for-word.

The eBook edition of this book is meant to be a living document, and as an eBook the notes, maps, and pictures can be easily added to or corrected and the author would appreciate contributions from readers and historians. Please email ljmartin@ljmartin.com with suggestions or corrections.

Edward Fitzerald Beale (middle age)

Beale ended his career as minister to Austria-Hungary.

Beale (in costume to cross Mexico)

Camels packed with up to 750 pounds

Dromedary

Bactrian

Edward Fitzgerald Beale

The Camel Expedition

Edward Fitzgerald Beale is an American icon, a quintessential man of the Manifest Destiny era. Naval hero, explorer, adventurer, scientist, surveyor are only a small portion of his talents and accomplishments. He was also a humaniterian, a rancher who completed the largest stock drive in the American west, and eventually a diplomat.

This volume, however, concerns itself with an accomplishment for which he was best known, and only then because it was unusual—camels in the American west.

The format of this book is unique in that it displays his report to Congress by scans of the actual pages of that report. You'll note that the text occasionally seems to wander a bit, to even slightly change size. That's the result of trying to maintain the integrity of a valuable historical document, trying to avoid busting the binding by holding it flat. It is, however, totally legible and should be of inestimable interest to true historians.

To add interest and information the pages are interlaces with notes, more contemporary maps, explanations, and photographs. It's the hope you'll complete the book with an intimate knowledge of this fascinating, historically significant slice of the taming of the American west, and of a very small part of the adventure and accomplishment of America's most unsung and succsesful characters.

Beale was born to a prominent Naval family in 1822 while. His family was living just a mile and a half north of the Capitol Building in Washington D.C. His maternal grandfather Thomas Truxtun was a captain in our early Navy, appointed by Washington. His paternal grandfather Georg Beale won a silver medal for allantry and good conduct and service on Lake Champlain during the war of 1812. So when the family came upon hard times and the cost of a proper education was out of the question, Beale had no compunction against applying for and receiving an appointment as a midshipman. He'd received his education aboard a frigate. Learning navigation would serve him well in later adventures, including the surveying of this wagon road.

He served with distinction, finally becoming ship's master of the USS Consttution, under Commodore Stockton. During the Mexican War, and the invasion of General Kearny into Mexican California, Beale was sent ashore to assist Kearny, and became the hero of the Battle of San Pasqual. There he met a lifelong friend, scout Kit Carson. Carson later said of Beale and his exploits, "I can't believe this guy, Ned Beale."

It was an untimate compliment, coming from one of America's most accomplished scouts and adventurers.

Beale made an earlier crossing (The Beale-Heap Expedition, 1853) under the employ of Secretary of the Interior Robert McCelland, ordered to proceed by the most expeditious route. He was instructed to locate possible sites for Indian reservations. He chose to diviate from the well-known trails, the Santa Fe and the Oregon trails, and to explore unknown territory. Rather than follow existing trails, leaving Westport Landing on the Missouri River, he headed directly west. He was no neophyte to the journey as this was his 7th trip to California. The one entry of that trip that stood out to me was Beale describing a hunt he went on with some Indians he'd encountered, Utes, he reported. His admiration for them here: "…but God forbid that I should ever hunt with such Indians again! I thought I had seen something of rough riding before, but all my experience faded before today's feats. Some places which we ascended it seemed to me that even a wildcat could hardly have passed over. Yet their well trained horses took them as part of the sport, and never made a misstep or blunder during the entire day…"

So he was well prepared for another crossing. As we follow Beale across the country from San Antonio, Texas, where he'd pick up some of his camels and Turks as they were called, north to Fort Defiance, New Mexico Territory, then west to Fort Tejon, California, we'll continue to comment on Beale's past, his accomplishments, and his location relative to contemporary cities, river names, landmarks, and other identifying marks.

We'll also comment on the flora, fauna and geography. And upon the tribes, which we can only presume by their location.

Scanned pages are from the actual report to Congress, added are my comments, maps, etc., those are not contained in the report.

For a look at Ned Beale and the first half of his exciting life, I invite you to pick up an ebook or paperback of my biographical novel RUSH TO

DESTINY, available on Amazon. Click on the title or the cover to go to that

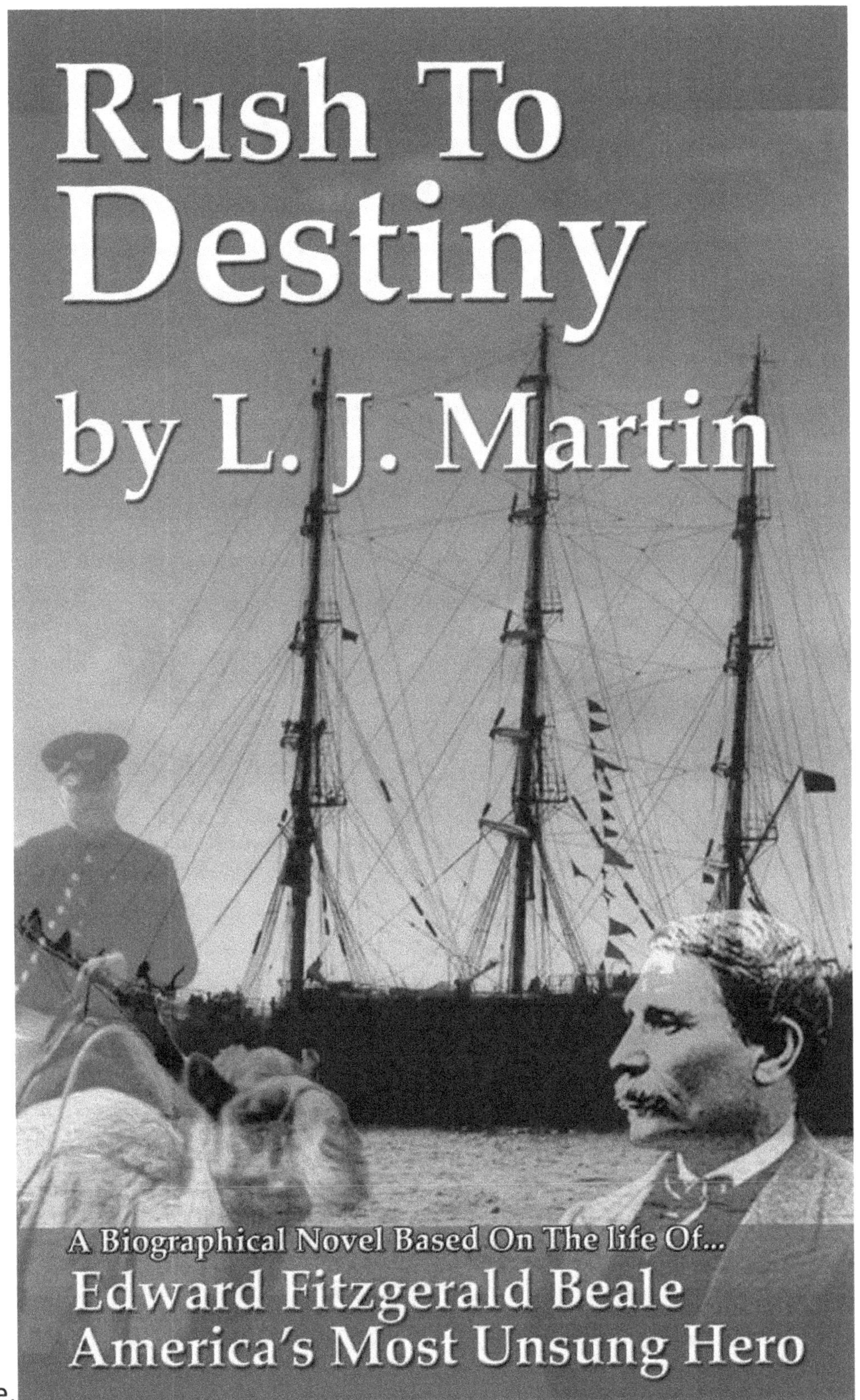

site.

WAGON ROAD FROM FORT DEFIANCE TO THE COLORADO RIVER.

LETTER

FROM

THE SECRETARY OF WAR,

TRANSMITTING

The report of the superintendent of the wagon road from Fort Defiance to the Colorado river.

MAY 12, 1858.—Ordered to be printed.

WAR DEPARTMENT,
Washington, May 10, 1858.

SIR: Referring to my letter of the 24th ultimo, in relation to the report of Edward F. Beale, esq., superintendent of the wagon road from Fort Defiance to the Colorado river, I have now the honor to transmit a copy of said report and of the accompanying map.

Very respectfully, your obedient servant,

JOHN B. FLOYD,
Secretary of War.

Hon. JAMES L. ORR,
Speaker of the House of Representatives.

WASHINGTON, *April* 26, 1858.

SIR: I have the honor to transmit herewith my daily journal of the survey made last summer and winter of a wagon road from Fort Defiance to the Colorado river or State line of California, near the 35th parallel. With this journal I send also an itinerary from Albuquerque, in New Mexico, to California. This itinerary gives distances as they exist, no air lines or imaginary curves, but every turn of our wheels recorded by the odometer attached. Latitudes and longitudes of almost all the camps are given. It is proper that I should call your attention to the fact, that to go by Fort Defiance, and thence to Zuñi, our starting point, is an unnecessary loss of time and a very great increase

Fort Defiance lays 35 miles northwest of present-day Albuquerque, New Mexico,
then Territory of New Mexico. Now just west of the Arizona/New Mexico border
in Arizona. The fort was established in 1851 as a base from which to control the
Navajo tribe. It was the first Army fort in what is now Arizona. It was abandoned
in 1861, then reoccupied in 1863 by troops under then Colonel Kit Carson. It was
abandoned again in 1864 at the conclusion of the Navajo Campaign. It became
the Navajo Indian Agency later in 1864 and continues to serve as such.

It's of note that Beale gave Aubrey and Whipple, his predecessors in crossing
nearly the same country, credit for same.

Francois Xavier Aubry (spelling differs), was a well-established trader on the Santa
Fe Trail when (1852) he decided to take a caravan down the Rio Grande and Gila
Rivers to California, arriving with over three thousand sheep. He returned crossing
the Tejon Pass and north of William's Mountain, south of the Grand Canyon,
approximately the same route as Beale's road. During that trip they were
attacked by a large party of Indians, probably Mojave, killing several but not until
nearly every man in his party was wounded. He made a second trip. In late 1853
he set out, arriving in Los Angeles in January 1854. His return to Albuquerque with
60 men in his party was uneventful. Just after arriving he was killed in a fight. His
dairy was found in his saddlebags and published, eliciting great interest in his
routes by those wanting a route to California.

Amil Weeks Whipple was a West Point graduate who worked on the Mexico/USA
boundary commission before being appointed to conduct a Pacific Railroad
Survey. The route was to originate in Fort Smith Arkansas to Los Angeles. He

employed frontiersman Antoine Leroux as a guide. They crossed the Texas

Panhandle, and the Mojave Desert, reaching Los Angeles in March of 1854.

of distance to no purpose. Complying with my instructions, however, I proceeded to Fort Defiance, and thence to Zuñi, but my train I sent by the direct road from the Gallo river to Zuñi, saving not less than sixty miles. Accompanying my journal is a table showing the thermometer at its highest elevation and lowest depression during the day on our outward journey in the months of September and October, and another kept on my return in January and February for the same purpose. A comparison of the two established the interesting fact, that one may travel the road in winter and summer without suffering the extremes of heat or cold. The journal which I send you is a faithful history of each day's work, written at the camp fire at the close of every day. I have not altered or changed it in any respect whatever, as I desired to speak of the country as it impressed me on the spot, so as to be as faithful in my description of it as possible. You will therefore find it very rough, but I hope those who may follow in my footsteps over the road may find it correct in every particular. I have written it for the use of emigrants more than for show, and if it answers the purpose of assisting them I shall be well satisfied. I have described things as I found them in the seasons in which I passed ; more or less water in the summer, more or less snow in winter, may be found by those who follow me. I am not responsible for the seasons, but I am for all my statements in relation to the country over which we passed. As far as the San Francisco mountain the road needs scarcely any other improvement than a few bridges. In one place alone a bridge at the Cañon Diablo would save twenty-five or thirty-five miles' travel, and on the whole road its length might be shortened by subsequent explorations and by straightening elbows one hundred miles. As this will inevitably become the great emigrant road to California, as well as that by which all stock from New Mexico will reach this place, it is proper that the government should put it in such a condition as to relieve the emigrant and stock drivers of as many of the hardships incident to their business as possible. For this purpose I would recommend that water dams be constructed at short intervals over the entire road. With these and a few bridges and military posts I do not doubt that the whole emigration to the Pacific coast would pursue this one line, instead of being divided and scattered over a half a dozen different routes. The advantage to the traveller, and the economy to the government of having one line instead of a dozen to protect, would fully repay all the expenses attending the construction of the road. I presume there can be no further question as to the practicability of the country near the thirty-fifth parallel for a wagon road, since Aubrey, Whipple, and myself, have all travelled it successfully with wagons, neither of us in precisely the same line, and yet through very much the same country. You will find by my journal that we encamped sometimes without wood and sometimes without water, but never without abundant grass. Starting with a drove of three hundred and fifty sheep, that number was increased by births upon the road, but not one was lost during the journey. In our first journey we groped, as it were, in the dark, and the weather being warm, did not care to leave the valleys for the wood, which is generally found on the hill-sides : and it is particularly worthy of

Roads were expected to have a source of potable water at no less than every 20 miles. Beale suggested that dams be constructed to contain water on obvious seasonal stream beds when natural year-round sources exceeded that distance.

He also suggested the establishment of a military fort where his road crossed the Colorado River.

From Wikipedia: **Beale's Crossing**, was a river crossing of the Colorado River, near the head of the Mohave Valley, between New Mexico Territory (now Arizona) and California along the along the 35th Parallel route of Beale's Wagon Road. The crossing was located at what became the site of Fort Mohave in what is now Fort Mohave, Arizona and west of Beaver Lake, Nevada. The crossing was named for Edward Fitzgerald Beale who lead the expedition that built what came to be called Beale's Wagon Road from Albuquerque, New Mexico to Beale's Crossing in California, then by way of the Mohave Trail/Old Spanish Trail, and another old route west from the Mojave River to Fort Tejon, California.

He closes his cover letter with a request for another $100,000.00 additional exploration to "cut off elbows" and to "straighten the road from point to point." Page 10 shows his road as surveyed.

Pay no attention to the page numbers on scanned pages.

note, that all the waters discovered were directly on the line of the road, and found almost without search and at short distances apart.

It is not to be questioned, that if so much was discovered on the first journey, a great deal more remains to be found upon a little exploration.

In preference to artesian wells, I propose to supply a deficiency of water by a system of dams across ravines and cañons, such as are used in Mexico and in portions of the State of Virginia, abundant evidences existing throughout the country that rains fall in sufficient quantities during the year to keep them full. In Mexico dams of this kind are used in the irrigation of large tracts of territory, which are dependent entirely upon this means for the supply of that element and for their crops. I cannot too urgently call your attention to this method of procuring abundant supplies of water, not only on the road to California, but on other emigrant routes where water may be scarce; it has the advantage over other artificial means of obtaining water, of returning a certainty for the expenditure of money, and of answering every purpose to be expected of wells of any kind, to say nothing of its being more economical.

In the journey of the year, during which I have been engaged upon this work, I have not lost a man, nor was there the slightest case of sickness in camp; the medicine chest proved only an incumbrance. My surgeon having left me, at the commencement of the journey, I did not employ, nor did I have need of one on the entire road. Even in midwinter, and on the most elevated portions of the road, not a tent was spread, the abundant fuel rendering them unnecessary for warmth and comfort.

I regard the establishment of a military post on the Colorado river as an indispensable necessity for the emigrant over this road; for, although the Indians, living in the rich meadow lands, are agricultural, and consequently peaceable, they are very numerous, so much so that we counted 800 men around our camp on the second day after our arrival on the banks of the river. The temptation of scattered emigrant parties with their families, and the confusion of inexperienced teamsters, rafting so wide and rapid a river with their wagons and families, would offer too strong a temptation for the Indians to withstand.

Another appropriation of $100,000, to build bridges, cut off elbows, and to straighten the road from point to point, and make other improvements and explorations, will be required for the present year.

I feel assured that the public lands, which would be brought into the market and sold within three years after the opening of this road, will repay four-fold the appropriation asked.

I have the honor to be, very respectfully, your obedient servant,

E. F. BEALE,
Superintendent.

Hon. JOHN B. FLOYD,
Secretary of War.

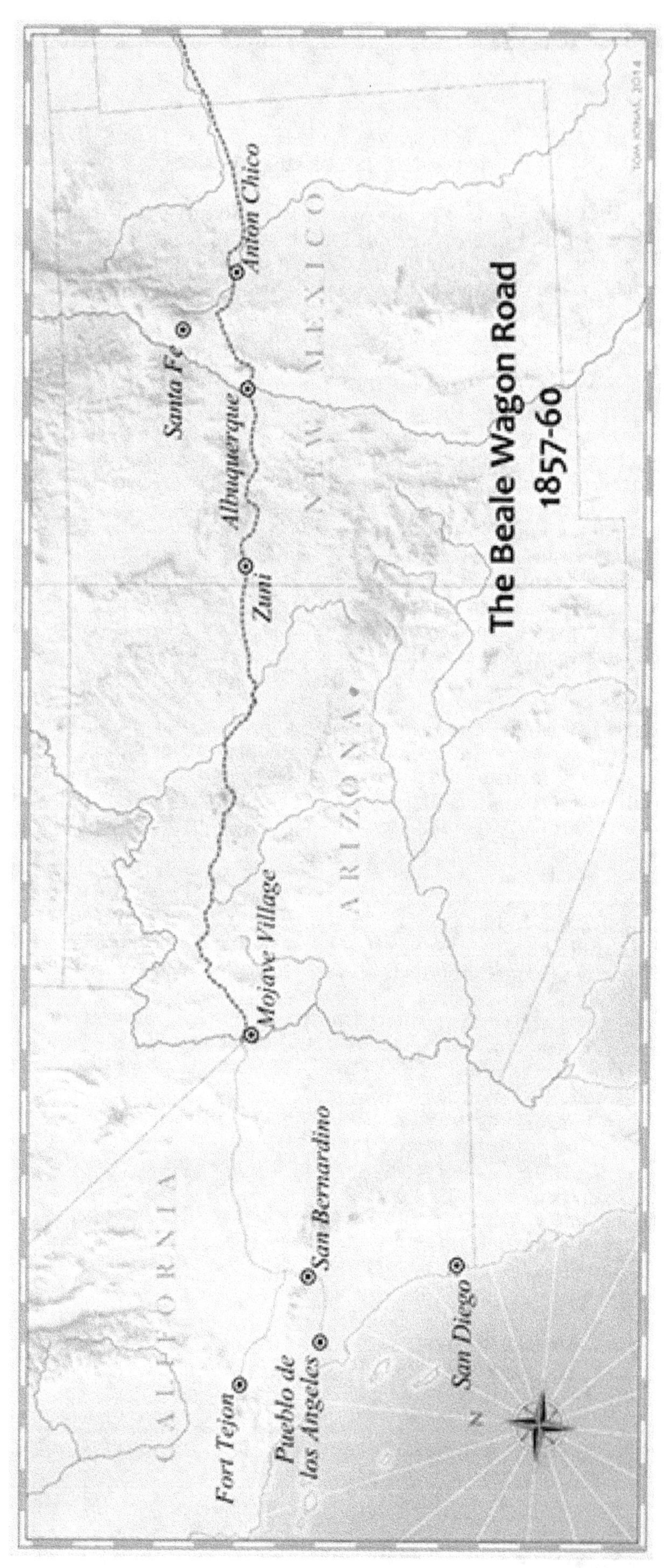

The Beale Wagon Road
1857-60
Anton Chico
Santa Fe
Albuquerque
Zuni
NEW MEXICO
ARIZONA
Mojave Village
CALIFORNIA
Fort Tejon
Pueblo de
los Angeles
San Bernardino
San Diego
N

Camps.	Viameter distance, in miles, from—		Latitude.	Longitude.	Remarks.
	Last camp.	Albuquerque.	° ′ ″	° ′ ″	
Albuquerque			35 05 51 N.	106 37 52 W.	Wood, water and grass.
Atrisco	2.10	2.10	35 04 56	106 38 52	Do. do.
Rio Puerco	20.63	22.73	35 02 56	106 56 20	Water in pools, wood and grass.
Near Puta	19.41	42.14	35 03 06	107 14 23	Abundance of wood, water and grass.
Covera	13.12	55.26	35 05 22	107 26 21	Water and grass abundant; wood scarce.
Hay Camp	13.06	68.32	35 04 32	107 39 12	Wood, water and grass plenty.
Agua Trio	25.37	93.69	35 01 36	107 58 20	Do. do.
Inscription Rock	16.28	109.97	35 02 41	108 14 21	Small spring; grass and wood plenty.
Ojo del Pescado	16.32	126.29	35 07 05	108 27 54	Water and grass plenty ; wood for camp use.
Zuñi	15.13	141.42	35 04 03	108 42 45	Wood scarce; grass and water abundant.
Indian Well	6.19	147.61			Wood, water and grass.
No. 1	14.43	162.04	35 04 01	109 01 48	Wood and grass; no water.
Jacob's Well	11.93	173.97	35 03 54	109 14 06	Water and grass ; wood for camp.
No. 2, Navajo Spring	6.57	180.54	35 06 10	109 20 10	Do. do.
Noon halt	13.62	194.16			Water by digging; grass and wood scarce.
No. 3	6.13	200.29	35 03 05	109 37 50	Grass abundant.
Noon halt	7.75	208.04			Wood, water and grass abundant.
No. 4	7.25	215.29	35 03 23	109 50 47	Water in holes; grass abundant; fuel sufficient.
Three Lakes	3.60	218.89			Water and grass abundant; fuel sufficient.
Crossing Puerco	1.75	220.64			Wood, water and grass abundant.
No. 5	11.25	231.89	34 53 10	110 05 15	Do. do.
No. 6	18.50	850.39	34 58 30	110 18 30	Do. do.
No. 7	10.17	260.56	34 58 20	110 28 05	Do. do.
No. 8	13.25	273.81	35 06 17	110 37 54	Do. do.
Cañon Diablo	19.35	293.16	35 17 50	110 52 58	Do. do.
No. 10	14.75	307.91	35 18 27	111 06 04	Do. do.
Near Cosnino Caves	13.50	321.41	35 15 58	111 20 30	Do. do.
Near San Francisco Spring	17.32	338.73	35 13 02	111 32 15	Do. do.
Leroux Spring	9.06	347.79	35 16 48	111 40 17	Do. do.
No. 13	8.48	356.27	35 18 02	111 48 15	Wood and grass; no water.

These "Itinerary" pages show:

Name of that day's camp

Distance from last camp

Distance from beginning at Albuquerque

Latitude

Longitude

Remarks: Such as availability of wood, water and grass (fodder for animals)

ITINERARY—Continued.

Camps.	Viameter distance, in miles, from—		Latitude.	Longitude.	Remarks.
	Last camp.	Albuquerque.			
			o ′ ″	o ′ ″	
Breckenridge Spring	11.13	367.40	35 20 30	111 57 10	Wood, water and grass abundant.
No. 14	8.07	375.49	35 20 10	112 01 21	Do. do.
Cedar Spring	6.50	381.97	35 22 08	112 07 30	Do. do.
No. 15	10.50	392.47	35 23 17	112 17 43	Do. do.
Alexander's Cañon	19.75	412.22	35 20 32	112 35 28	Wood and grass abundant; not much water.
Smith's Spring	8.05	420.27	35 19 45	112 42 53	Wood, water and grass abundant.
Pass Dornin	8.75	429.02	85 13 05	112 45 17	Wood and grass abundant; no water.
No. 19	13.50	442.52	35 16 19	112 58 11	Do. do.
No. 20	16.35	458.87	35 20 37	113 12 08	Water 2 miles from camp; wood and grass abundant.
Hemphell's Spring	4.06	....	35 22 18	113 16 57	Abundant wood, water and grass.
No. 21	21.25	480.12	35 20 17	113 35 40	Do. do.
No. 22	9.75	489.87	35 26 01	113 43 32	Wood and grass abundant; spring one mile distant.
No. 23	5.50	495.37	35 25 59	113 48 10	Wood and grass abundant; no water.
No. 24	8.45	503.82	35 21 38	113 56 17	Wood and grass; spring 3 miles distant.
No. 25	16.75	520.57	35 13 26	114 08 20	Wood and grass; no water.
Sabadras Spring	7.25	527.82	35 09 12	114 11 25	Wood, water and grass.
No. 26	13.25	541.07	35 05 25	114 16 30	Wood; no water or grass.
Spring	8.75	549.82	35 02 08	114 22 36	Wood, water and grass.
No. 27	1.25	551.07	35 02 56	114 23 17	Do. do.
No. 28	3.17	554.24	35 03 39	114 25 42	Do. do.
No. 29	1.25	555.49	35 04 11	114 26 10	Do. do.
No. 30	3.11	558.60	35 05 56	114 28 25	Do. do.
East Bank, No. 31	3.25	561.85	35 04 27	114 31 19	Colorado river; wood.
West Bank, No. 32	....	....	35 04 58	114 32 41	Water and grass abundant.

Respectfully,

E. F. BEALE, *Superintendent, &c.*

Approved:

C. E. THORBURN, *Lieut. U. S. N., and A. S. S. N.*

E. F. BEALE, *Superintendent, &c.*

The chart opposite shows the date and daily temperatures in Fahrenheit but taken at different times of the day, depending upon when they left or arrived in camp. However, it's a close estimate of the highs and lows of the day.

Temperature indicated by thermometer (Fahrenheit) at different periods of the day, en route west, from Zuñi to Colorado river, from September 1, 1857, to October 19, 1857, inclusive.

Date.	Temperature.		Date.	Temperature.	
	Highest.	Lowest.		Highest.	Lowest.
1857.	°	°	1857.	°	°
September 1	84. 5	60	September 26	90	48
2	80	56	27	89	45
3	68. 5	54. 5	28	83	62
4	82	55	29	83	45
5	88	60. 5	30	80	57
6	83	65	October 1	74. 5	47
7	91. 5	53	2	65	55
8	87	58	3	76. 5	58
9	89	58	4	83	51
10	77	55	5	85	51
11	79	51	6	74	66
12	74	47	7	72	46
13	78	38	8	81	46
14	80	59	9	68	44
15	87	42	10	70. 5	57
16	82. 5	61	11	73. 5	43. 5
17	82. 5	62	12	71	42
18	84	62	13	79	68. 5
19	85	40	14	82	48. 5
20	84	50	15	86. 5	70. 5
21	77	69	16	76	70
22	82	69	17	82	70
23	88. 5	56. 5	18	82	58
24	87. 5	48. 5	19	81. 5	48
25	85. 5	52. 5			

These readings are at different hours, commencing when all hands were called in the morning, and exhibit the extreme heat and cold of the day.

E. F. BEALE, *Superintendent, &c.*

This chart shows temps at 4 am, 12 noon, and 6 pm.

Temperature indicated by thermometer (Fahrenheit) at different periods of the day, viz: 4 o'clock a. m., 12 m., and 6 p. m., en route east, from the Colorado river to the " Ojo del Gallo," from January 25 to February 21, inclusive.

Day.	Temperature.		
	4 o'clock a. m.	12 o'clock m.	6 o'clock p. m.
	°	°	°
January 25	32	50	32
26	40	53	38
27	39	54	45
28	34	58	43
29	34	76	50
30	31	75	40
31	31	61	50
February 1	33	71	48
2	33	39	49
3	29	36	30
4	29	48	57
5	18	67	35
6	27	70	37
7	33	67	51
8	25	58	45
9	31	58	45
10	31	51	45
11	32	53	45
12	28	45	42
13	28	55	48
14	25	51	31
15	25	75	38
16	24	58	33
17	26	53	32
18	28	59	35
19	30	70	32
20	30	50	30
21	35	61	37

E. F. BEALE, *Superintendent, &c.*

The next 7 pages are detailed meteorological observations showing, at a given time, temperature, barometric pressure, wind force and direction, and cloud cover.

Meteorological observations taken on the reconnoissance of the wagon road from Fort Defiance to the Colorado.

No. of camp.	Date.	Hour.	Thermometer		Barometer	Wind		Clouds.
			Attached.	Detached.		Force.	Direction.	
			°	°	Inches.			
	1857. Aug. 31	9 a.m.	75.5	70.5	21.182	2	East	Cir. stra
Station 1	do.	11.30 a.m.	89.5	91	24.260	0		do.
2	do.	12.30 p.m.	89	85	21.107	0		do.
3	do.	1 p.m.	89	93	24.206	1	East	.....
4	do.	1.30 p.m.	89	98	24.184	1	do.	Nimbus
5	do.	2.45 p.m.	94.5	95.5	24.194	2	do.	do.
6	do.	2 p.m.	93.5	95.5	24.200	0	Calm	do.
7	do.	2.15 p.m.	92.5	96.5	24.184	0	do.	do.
8	do.	2.30 p.m.	98.5	91.5	24.192	1	N.W	do.
9	do.	3 p.m.	96.5	92	21.186	1	do.	do.
10	do.	3.30 p.m.	85	79	24.084	2	do.	do.
11	do.	3.45 p.m.	85	83	23.980	3	North	Cir. cum
12	do.	4 p.m.	87	86	23.984	3	do.	do.
13	do.	4.30 p.m.	87	80	23.976	3	do.	do.
14	do.	5 p.m.	78.5	71.5	23.806	2	do.	Cum
A	do.		73.5	71.5	23.890	2	do.	Nimbus
15	do.	5.30 p.m.	71.5	69	23.800	2	S.W	Cir. Stra
16	do.	6 p.m.	70.5	67	23.902	1	do.	do.
17	do.	6.30 p.m.	67.5	68	23.982	1	West	do.
Camp 1	do.	7 p.m.	55	56.5	23.982	0	Calm	do.
1	Sept. 1	5 a.m.	55	56.5	23.994	0	do.	do.
Station 2	do.	6 a.m.	58.5	58	24.082	0	do.	do.
3	do.	7 a.m.	61.5	58.5	24.064	0	do.	do.
4	do.	7.30 a.m.	62.5	60	23.964	1	East	Cir. cum
5	do.	8 a.m.	66.5	65.5	24.260	1	do.	do.
6	do.	9.30 a.m.	74.5	71.5	24.406	2	South	do.
7	do.	10 a.m.	75.5	73.5	24.482	2	do.	Cum. stra
8	do.	10.30 a.m.	82.5	75	24.386	0	Calm	Cir. cum
9	do.	10.45 a.m.	80	76	24.460	Jacob's	do.	do.
10	do.	11 a.m.	77.5	78	24.584	Well.	do.	do.
11	do.	3 p.m.	81	80.5	24.374	0	do.	do.
12	do.	3.30 p.m.	84.5	81.5	24.372	0	West	Cir. stra
13	do.	4 p.m.	82	77	24.290	1	do.	do.
14	do.	4.30 p.m.	76	74.5	24.391	1	W.S.W	do.
15	do.	4.45 p.m.	77.5	75.5	24.306	2	do.	Cum. stra
16	do.	5 p.m.	75.5	73.8	24.386	2	do.	do.
17	do.	6 p.m.	71	67.5	24.606	2	do.	do.
Camp 2	do.	6.30 p.m.	67.5	66	24.590	2	do.	do.
2	Sept. 2	6 a.m.	56.5	56	24.664	1	West	do.
Station 1	do.	7 a.m.	59	56.5	24.690	1	do.	Nimbus
2	do.	8 a.m.	72.5	62.5	24.764	1	do.	do.
3	do.	9 a.m.	72.5	69	24.794	1	do.	Cum
4	do.	9.15 a.m.	74.5	69	24.692	1	do.	do.
5	do.	9.45 a.m.	72.5	68.5	24.660	1	Calm	do.
6	do.	9.52 a.m.	70.5	69	24.606	0	do.	Cir. cum
7	do.	10 a.m.	75.5	79	24.682	0	do.	do.
8	do.	10.30 a.m.	79	80	24.582	0	West	do.
9	do.	11 a.m.	78	73	24.784	1	S.W	do.
10	do.	12 m.	76.5	74.5	24.782	1	East	do.
11	do.	3 p.m.	69.5	68	24.770	1	do.	Cir. cum
12	do.	4 p.m.	69.5	67.5	24.670	1	do.	do.
13	do.	4.30 p.m.	69.5	65.5	24.696	2	North	.....
14	do.	5 p.m.	69.5	64	24.582	2	do.	Cir. cum
15	do.	6.30 p.m.	68.5	63	24.402	3	do.	.....
Camp 3	do.	7 p.m.	66	63.5	24.490	3	do.	.....
3	do.	8.30 p.m.	66.5	64	24.584	3	N.W	Cir. stra
3	Sept. 3	6 a.m.	54.5	54.5	24.570	2	do.	do.
Station 1	do.	9 a.m.	59.5	59.5	24.802	2	do.	do.
2	do.	10 a.m.	61.5	59.5	24.992	1	West	do.
3	do.	2.30 p.m.	68.5	65	24.690	1	Calm	Cir. cum
4	do.	3 p.m.	66.5	67.5	24.990	0	East	do.
Camp 4	do.	5 p.m.	68.5	67	25.062	1	do.	do.
4	do.	7 p.m.	60.5	60.5	25.060	1	do.	Cum. stra
4	Sept. 4	7 a.m.	53.5	55	25.060	1	do.	do.
Station 1	do.	8.30 a.m.	70.5	68	25.172	1	Calm	do.
2	do.	9.30 a.m.	84.5	74	25.272	0	East	do.
3	do.	12 m.	79.5	79.5	25.194	1	West	Stra
4	do.	3 p.m.	75.5	78.5	25.194	3	S.W	do.
5	do.	4 p.m.	77.5	82	25.162	4	do.	Cir. stra
6	do.	5 p.m.	78.5	82.5	25.190	2	East	do.
Camp 5	do.	7 p.m.	68.5	67.5	25.176	2	N E	Cum
5	Sept. 5	7 a.m.	62.5	60.5	25.366	3	do.	do.
Station 1	do.	8 a.m.	71	69.5	25.382	3		

METEOROLOGICAL OBSERVATIONS—Continued.

No. of camp.	Date.	Hour.	Thermometer.		Barometer	Wind.		Clouds.
			Attached.	Detached.		Force.	Direction.	
	1857.		°	°	Inches.			
Station..... 1	Sept. 5	9 a.m....	73.5	71.5	25.382	3	N.E.	Cir. stra. ......
1	....do....	12 m.....	79	79	25.382	5	East.....	....do......
2	....do....	1 p.m....	86.5	88	25.384	5	..do......	....do......
3	....do....	2 p.m....	81	80	25.300	4	..do......	....do......
4	....do....	3 p.m....	81.5	82.5	25.362	0	Calm	....do......
5	....do....	4 p.m....	83	79	25.384	0	..do......	....
Camp 6	....do....	5 p.m....	64.5	66	25.382	0	..do......	Cir. cum......
6	... do....	9 p.m....	58	59	25.402	2	S.W......	....do......
6	Sept. 6	5.30 a.m.	51.5	62	25.404	0	Calm	Cum. stra
Station..... 1	....do....	7 a.m....	70.5	71	25.494	1	S.W......	....do......
2	....do....	9 a.m....	70.5	70	25.491	0	Calm	....do......
3	... do....	12 m.....	78.5	73	25.474	0	..do......	Cir. stra
4	....do....	3 p.m....	77	77.5	25.482	0	..do......	....do......
Camp 7	....do....	5 p.m....	73	71.5	25.472	1	S.W......	....do......
7	.. .do....	7 p.m....	65	65	25.474	0	Calm	....do......
7	Sept. 7	5.30 a.m.	52.5	53.5	25.392	0	.do......	Cum. stra..
Station..... 1	...do....	7 a.m....	68.5	68	25.402	1	East.....	Cir. stra.
2	...do....	9 a.m....	80.5	75	25.494	2	..do......	....do......
3	...do....	12 m.....	80.5	83	25.496	2	N.E......	....do......
4	...do....	1 p.m	87.5	85	25.490	4	..do......	....do......
5	...do....	2 p m	92.5	91.5	25.400	2	..do......	....do......
6	...do....	3 p.m....	89.5	89.5	25.380	2	S.W......	....do......
7	...do ...	4 p.m....	86.5	89	25.496	2	..do......	... do......
Camp 8	....do....	5.30 p.m.	81.5	83	25.386	0	Calm	....do......
8	...do....	7 p.m....	75.5	77.5	25.362	0	..do......	Cum.
8	Sept. 8	5.30 a.m.	57.5	58	25.372	0	..do......	Cir. cum.
Station..... 1	....do....	7 a.m....	58	58	25.476	1	East.....	....do......
2	....do....	7 a.m....	69	63	25.406	1	..do......	....do......
3	....do....	8 a.m....	68	65	25.574	4	..do......	....do......
4	....do....	8.35 p.m.	80	76	25.500	4	..do......	Nimbus
5	....do....	9 a.m....	84	80	25.570	2	..do......	....do......
5	....do....	12 m.....	84	84	25.466	2	South....	Cir. cum.....
6	....do....	3 p.m....	87.5	87	25.596	2	..do......	....do......
7	....do....	4 p.m....	85	84	25.500	2	..do......	....do......
Camp 9	....do....	5 p.m....	78	78	28.494	3	..do......	....
9	....do	7 p.m....	77	76.5	25.496	3	..do......	Cir. cum.....
9	Sept. 9	6 a.m....	57.5	58	25.500	3	..do......	....do......
Station..... 1	....do....	7 a.m....	69.5	68.5	25.492	3	..do......	....do......
2	....do....	7.15 a.m.	68.5	66	25.466	....		....do......
2	....do....	9 a.m....	78.5	79	25.466	2	East.....	Cum. stra.....
3	....do....	12 m...	85.5	83	25.374	2	South....	....do......
4	....do....	12.30 p.m.	86.5	87.5	25.096	2	..do......	Cir. cum
5	.. ...do....	1 p.m....	85.5	84	24.994	3	S.W......	....do......
6	....do....	1.30 p.m.	86.5	82.5	25.002	3	..do......	Cir. cum. stra.
7	....do....	2 p.m....	87	87	24.992	3	..do......	....do......
8	....do....	2.30 p.m.	90	87	25.000	1	..do......	....do......
9	....do....	3 p.m....	77.5	74.5	24.762	6	West	Cir. cum
Camp .... .10	....do....	4 p.m....	75.5	75.5	24.674	2	..do......	Cir. stra. ......
10	....do....	7 p.m ...	66	68	24.682	2	..do......	....do......
10	Sept. 10	6 a.m....	55	55	24.576	4	S.W......	....do......
Station..... 1	....do...	7 a.m....	69	65	24.500	4	..do......	....do......
2	....do....	8 a.m....	70	69.5	24.400	5	..do......	....do......
3	....do....	8.15 a.m.	70	69	24.462	5	..do	....do......
4	....do....	9 a.m....	76	74.5	24.466	5	..do......	....do......
5	....do....	10 a m ...	77	76	24.092	3	..do......	....do......
6	....do....	10.30 a.m.	77	76	23.972	3	..do......	....do......
7	....do. ...	10.45 a.m.	77	76.5	24.190	3	..do......	....do......
7	....do....	12 m... .	71	71.5	24.100	3	..do......	....do......
8	....do....	2 p.m....	74	73	23.902	3	South....	....do......
9	....do....	3 p.m....	76	77	24.000	3	..do......	Cir. cum
Camp 11	....do....	3.30 p.m.	74.5	76	24.000	4	S.W......	Cir. stra.....
11	....do....	7 p.m....	62	61.5	23.970	2	West	Cum. stra.....
11	Sept. 11	6 a.m....	50	51	23.902	0	Calm	...do......
Station..... 1	....do....	6.30 a.m.	57.5	57	23.863	0	..do......	...do......
2	....do....	7 a.m....	57	56	23.960	0	..do......	Cir. stra.
3	....do....	7.30 a.m.	63.5	64.5	23.900	2	N.W....	....do......
4	....do....	8 a.m....	68.5	67	23.782	2	..do......	....do......
5	. ..do....	9 a m ...	73.5	74	23.684	2	..do......	Cum
6	....do....	10 a m ...	70	71	23.594	3	..do......	....do......
7	....do....	11.45 a.m.	78.5	77	23.586	4	South ...	Cir. stra.
7	....do....	12 m.....	79.5	79	23.586	4	..do......	....do......
7	....do....	1 p.m....	72.5	70	23.592	5	..do......	....do......
8	....do ..	2 p.m....	73	75	23.302	5	..do......	....do......
9	....do....	2.30 p.m.	72.5	73	23.306	3	..do......	....do......
10	....do....	3 p.m....	67.5	66	23.194	3	..do......	Cir. cum
11	....do....	4 p.m....	71	71.5	23.304	3	S.W......	....do......

METEOROLOGICAL OBSERVATIONS—Continued.

No. of camp.	Date.	Hour.	Thermometer.		Barometer	Wind.		Clouds.
			Attached.	Detached.		Force.	Direction.	
	1857.		°	°	Inches.			
Camp 12	Sept. 11	5.30 p.m.	65	67	23.364	4	S.W.	Cir. cum.
12	do	7 p.m.	60	62	23.358	4	do	Cir.
12	Sept. 12	7 a.m.	44	47	23.462	0	Calm	do
Station 1	do	9 a.m.	67.5	68	23.476	0	do	do
2	do	11 a.m.	74.5	76	23.386	0	do	do
3	do	12 m.	72.5	72	23.264	0	do	do
4	do	2 p.m.	73.5	74	22.975	2	East	Cum. stra.
4	do	2.15 p.m.	74	74	23.092	2	do	do
5	do	4.30 p.m.	67.5	68	23.075	2	do	Cir. cum. stra.
6	do	5 p.m.	65	64	22.962	3	do	do
7	do	6 p.m.	62.5	61.5	22.882	3	do	do
Camp 13	do	7 p.m.	62	62.5	22.800	1	do	do
13	Sept. 13	6 a.m.	37.5	38	22.862	0	Calm	Stra.
Station 1	do	7 a.m.	61	60	22.886	0	do	do
2	do	9 a.m.	73	73	23.166	0	do	Cir. stra.
3	do	10.30 a.m.	80	78	23.300	0	do	do
3	do	12 m.	71	72	23.290	0	do	do
4	do	3 p.m.	75	76.5	23.292	0	do	do
5	do	4 p.m.	74.5	73	23.252	0	do	do
Camp 14	do	5 p.m.	60	59.5	23.554	0	do	do
14	Sept. 14	5.30 a.m.	62.5	59.5	23.664	1	East	Cir. cum.
Station 1	do	7 a.m.	65.5	63	23.894	0	Calm	do
2	do	8 a.m.	65.5	63	23.886	0	do	Nimbus.
3	do	9 a.m.	79	80	24.100	0	do	do
3	do	12 m.	71	72.5	24.092	1	S.W.	do
4	do	1 p.m.	76	75	24.270	2	West	do
5	do	1.30 p.m.	69	67	24.100	2	do	do
6	do	3 p.m.	61.5	63	24.080	2	do	Cir. cum.
7	do	4 p.m.	61	61.5	24.252	1	do	Nimbus.
8	do	6 p.m.	70	70.5	24.380	0	Calm	Cir. cum.
Camp 15	do	7 p.m.	65.5	64	24.474	1	S.W.	do
15	Sept. 15	5.30 a.m.	42.5	42	24.494	2	do	Stra.
Station 1	do	6 a.m.	55	55.5	24.392	4	N.W.	do
2	do	7 a.m.	67	67	24.380	2	do	Cir. stra.
3	do	8 a.m.	67	67.5	24.452	0	Calm	do
4	do	9 a.m.	76	77	24.566	0	do	do
5	do	10 a.m.	85	87	24.656	0	do	do
6	do	12 m.	87	85	24.582	0	do	Nimbus.
6	do	1.30 p.m.	73	72	24.570	0	do	do
7	do	2 p.m.	73	71.5	24.540	1	East	Cir. stra.
8	do	3 p.m.	70	72	24.486	1	do	Cir. cum.
9	do	3.15 p.m.	71.5	71	24.552	3	do	do
10	do	3.30 p.m.	68.5	67	24.656	4	do	do
11	do	4 p.m.	68	68	24.490	4	do	do
12	do	5 p.m.	68	69	24.460	4	do	do
13	do	6 p.m.	62	63	24.596	3	N.E.	do
Camp 16	do	7 p.m.	60	60.5	24.670	3	do	do
King's Creek	do	6 p.m.	62	63	24.595	2	do	Cir. stra.
Do	do	7 p.m.	60	60.5	24.670	2	do	Cir. cum. strn.
Do	Sept. 16	9 a.m.	61	61	24.654	2	do	do
Do	do	12 m.	70.5	71	24.652	3	South	do
Do	do	3 p.m.	66	64.5	24.654	3	do	do
Do	do	7 p.m.	63	62	24.650	4	do	Cir. stra.
Do	Sept. 17	7 a.m.	58	57	24.600	4	do	do
Do	do	9 a.m.	61.5	61	24.654	2	do	do
Do	do	12 m.	70	69	24.670	0	Calm	Cir. cum.
Do	do	3 p.m.	82	71.5	24.590	0	do	do
Do	do	5 p.m.	63	61	24.632	0	do	do
Do	do	7 p.m.	60	60	24.690	1	East	do
Do	Sept. 18	7 a.m.	62	62	24.690	2	do	Cum. stra.
Do	do	9 a.m.	70	69	24.860	3	do	do
Do	do	12 m.	83	83	25.000	4	do	do
Do	do	12.30 p.m.	80.5	82	24.862	4	do	do
Do	do	1 p.m.	82	83	24.764	4	do	Cum.
Do	do	2 p.m.	84	84	24.688	0	Calm	do
Do	do	3 p.m.	81	83	24.782	0	do	do
Do	do	4 p.m.	82	84	24.688	0	do	do
Do	do	7 p.m.	71	71.5	24.782	2	East	do
Do	Sept. 19	6 a.m.	40	40	24.562	2	do	do
Do	do	7 a.m.	60	61	24.750	5	do	Cir. cum.
Do	do	8 a.m.	69	70.5	24.552	5	do	do
Do	do	9 a.m.	83	82	24.562	3	do	do
Do	do	9.30 a.m.	82	81.5	24.454	3	do	Cum. stra.
Do	do	10 a.m.	82.5	82	24.484	1	do	Cir. cum.
Do	do	10.30 a.m.	84	85	24.394	1	do	do
Obs. lost	Sept. 20	....	....	....	25.060	....	....	Cum.

METEOROLOGICAL OBSERVATIONS—Continued.

No. of camp.	Date	Hour	Attached (°)	Detached (°)	Barometer (Inches)	Force	Direction	Clouds
Obs. lost......	Sept. 21				25.064			Cum.
King's Creek..	Sept. 22	7 a.m	69.5	69	25.062	2	N.E.	Cir. cum
Do	do	8 a.m	76	75.5	25.068	2	..do	Cum. stra
Do	do	9 a.m	69	70.5	25.068	3	..do	...do
Do	do	10 a.m	75.5	76	25.070	3	..do	...do
Do	do	11 a.m	78	77	25.066	3	..do	Cir. stra
Do	do	12 m	81	82	24.984	2	..do	...do
Do	do	1 p.m	80.5	82	24.992	2	..do	...do
Do	do	2 p.m	87	88.5	24.996	5	..do	...do
Do	do	3 p.m	88	91.5	24.998	5	..do	Cum.
Do	do	4 p.m	86	89	24.996	2	..do	...do
Do	do	5 p.m	83.5	82	24.988	0	Calm	Cir. stra
Do	Sept. 23	7 a.m	56	56.5	24.866	1	N.E.	...do
Do	do	8 a.m	67	66.5	24.862	1	..do	...do
Do	do	9 a.m	79	78	24.866	3	..do	...do
Do	do	10 a.m	76.5	78	24.886	3	..do	Cir. cum
Do	do	11 a.m	83.5	82.2	24.886	3	..do	...do
Do	do	12 m	84	88.5	24.850	2	S.W.	...do
Do	do	1 p.m	82.5	83	24.884	2	..do	...do
Do	do	2 p.m	84.5	84	24.874	2	..do	...do
Do	do	3 p.m	84.5	63.5	24.870	2	..do	...do
Do	do	4 p.m	86.5	86	24.796	2	..do	...do
Do	do	5 p.m	84.5	84.5	24.782	2	..do	...do
Do	do	6 p.m	79	78	24.766	2	..do	...do
Do	do	7 p.m	70	71.5	24.772	2	..do	...do
Do	Sept. 24	7 a.m	44	48.5	24.784	2	..do	...do
Do	do	8 a.m	59.5	59.5	24.880	2	South	Cir. stra
Do	do	10 a.m	79.5	81.5	24.874	2	..do	...do
Do	do	11 a.m	89.5	87.5	24.874	2	..do	...do
Do	do	12 m	84	81.5	24.861	2	..do	...do
Do	do	1 p.m	84	84.5	24.800	1	..do	...do
Do	do	2 p.m	81.5	84	24.800	1	..do	...do
Do	do	3 p.m	86.5	85	24.796	1	..do	...do
Do	do	4 p.m	85.5	86	24.792	1	..do	Cum.
Do	do	5 p.m	82.5	81.5	24.784	0	Calm	...do
Do	do	6 p.m	87.5	86	24.766	0	..do	Cir. cum
Do	do	7 p.m	63	60	24.856	0	..do	...do
Do	Sept. 25	7 a.m	51	52	24.856	0	..do	...do
Do	do	8 a.m	54.5	56.5	24.860	0	..do	...do
Do	do	9 a.m	73	77	24.850	0	..do	...do
Do	do	10 a.m	78.5	77	24.892	0	..do	...do
Do	do	11 a.m	83	81	24.886	0	..do	...do
Do	do	12 m	84	84	24.820	0	..do	...do
Do	do	1 p.m	82	83.5	24.886	1	N.E.	...do
Do	do	2 p.m	84.5	83	24.862	1	..do	...do
Do	do	3 p.m	85.5	85.5	24.862	1	..do	Cir. cum. stra
Do	do	4 p.m	83.5	85	24.870	1	..do	...do
Do	do	5 p.m	85	87	24.800	1	..do	Cir. stra
Do	do	6 p.m	79.5	81	24.802	0	Calm	...do
Do	do	7 p.m	70	69	24.788	0	..do	...do
Do	Sept. 26	7 a.m	50.5	43	24.796	0	..do	Cum.
Do	do	8 a.m	55	54	24.874	0	..do	...do
Do	do	9 a.m	62	60.5	24.896	0	..do	Cir. cum
Do	do	10 a.m	76	74.5	24.896	0	..do	...do
Do	do	11 a.m	86.5	86	24.895	0	..do	Cum. stra
Do	do	12 m	86.5	86	24.902	0	..do	...do
Do	do	1 p.m	84.5	82	24.900	1	N.E.	...do
Do	do	2 p.m	90	90	24.876	3	..do	...do
Do	do	3 p.m	88	88	24.876	3	..do	Cir. stra
Do	do	4 p.m	83.5	85	24.874	3	..do	...do
Do	do	5 p.m	83.5	82	24.878	1	..do	...do
Do	do	6 p.m	80.5	79	24.850	0	Calm	...do
Do	do	7 p.m	72	69	24.960	0	..do	...do
Do	Sept. 27	7 a.m	43	45	24.960	0	..do	...do
Do	do	8 a.m	54	55	24.900	1	S.E.	Cir. cum
Do	do	9 a.m	68.5	69	24.900	1	..do	...do
Do	do	10 a.m	80	76	24.000	1	..do	...do
Do	do	11 a.m	83	83	24.902	1	..do	...do
Do	do	12 m	82	82	24.860	1	..do	...do
Do	do	1 p.m	87	84	24.060	2	..do	Cum. stra
Do	do	2 p.m	89	83	24.894	2	..do	...do
Do	do	3 p.m	89	83	24.000	3	..do	Cum.
Do	do	4 p.m	80	83	24.879	3	..do	...do
Do	do	5 p.m	73	72	24.870	3	..do	Cir. cum
Do	do	6 p.m	70	73	24.668	3	..do	Cum. stra
Do	do	7 p.m	70	72				

METEOROLOGICAL OBSERVATIONS—Continued.

No. of camp.	Date.	Hour.	Thermometer.		Barometer	Wind.		Clouds.
			Attached.	Detached.		Force.	Direction.	
	1857.		°	°	Inches.			
King's creek	Sept. 28	7 a.m	60	62	24.890	2	S.E	Cum. stra
Do	...do	8 a.m	74	74	24.000	2	..do	Cir. cum
Do	...do	9 a.m	75	80	24.000	2	..do	....do
Do	...do	10 a.m	73	75	24.860	2	..do	....do
Do	...do	11 a.m	80	82	24.000	2	..do	Cir. stra
Do	...do	12 m	80	83	24.986	2	..do	....do
Do	...do	1 p.m	80	76	24.860	2	S.S.W	....do
Do	...do	2 p.m	84	80	24.960	2	S.E	Cir. cum
Do	...do	3 p.m	83	72	24.920	2	..do	....do
Do	...do	4 p.m	77	79	24.789	3	..do	....do
Station 1	...do	5 p.m	76	79	24.811	3	..do	....do
2	...do	6 p.m	74	80	25.000	3	..do	Cir
3	...do	7 p.m	70	73	24.981	2	..do	....do
4	...do	7.30 p.m	68	68	24.860	1	Calm	Cir. cum
Camp	Sept. 29	5.30 a.m	40	45	.871	0	..do	....do
Do	...do	6 a.m	40	45	.876	0	..do	....do
Do	...do	7 a.m	41	45	.872	0	..do	....do
Do	...do	8 a.m	43	45	.873	0	..do	....do
Do	...do	9 a.m	45	43	.876	0	South	....do
Do	...do	10 a.m	56	50	.876	1	..do	....do
Do	...do	10.15 a.m	78	55	.973	1	.....	....do
Do	...do	10.45 a.m	76	63	25.000	1	South	....do
Do	...do	11 a.m	76	65	.871	2	..do	....do
Do	...do	11.15 a.m	79	63	.868	2	..do	....do
Do	...do	11.45 a.m	79	64	.840	2	..do	....do
Do	...do	12.15 p.m	76	67	25.000	2	..do	....do
Do	...do	1 p.m	83	85	24.860	3	..do	....do
Alexander's Cañon	...do	2 p.m	83	85	24.600	3	..do	....do
Do	...do	3 p.m	84	81	24.580	2	..do	....do
Do	...do	4 p.m	76	79	24.570	0	Calm	....do
Do	...do	5 p.m	74	73	24.571	0	..do	....do
Do	...do	6 p.m	75	71	24.620	1	S.E	....do
Do	...do	7 p.m	69	58	24.680	1	..do	....do
Do	Sept. 30	6 a.m	40	39	24.590	2	..do	....do
Do	...do	7 a.m	63	57	24.590	2	..do	....do
Do	...do	8 a.m	62.5	60	24.589	0	Calm	....do
Do	...do	9 a.m	68	67	24.590	0	..do	....do
Do	...do	10 a.m	79	80	24.590	0	..do	....do
Do	...do	11 a.m	81	81	24.562	1	South	Cum. stra
Do	...do	12 m	78	76	24.590	1	..do	....do
Do	...do	1 p.m	78	76	24.571	2	..do	....do
Do	...do	2 p.m	77	73	24.610	2	..do	....do
Do	...do	3 p.m	78	75	24.481	2	..do	Cum
Do	...do	4 p.m	81	80	24.481	0	Calm	....do
Do	...do	5 p.m	76	71	24.470	1	N.E	....do
Do	...do	6 p.m	72	70.5	24.410	1	..do	....do
Do	...do	7 p.m	69	66	24.464	1	..do	Cir. cum
Do	Oct. 1	5 a.m	45	47	24.430	1	South	....do
Do	...do	6 a.m	46	46	24.383	1	..do	....do
Do	...do	7 a.m	61	57	24.290	3	S.E	....do
Do	...do	8 a.m	68	60	24.291	3	..do	Cir. stra
Do	...do	9 a.m	72	68	24.190	3	..do	....do
Do	...do	10 a.m	81	85	24.290	3	..do	Cir
Do	...do	11 a.m	79	78	24.263	3	N.W	....do
Do	...do	12 m	75	74.5	24.171	4	..do	Cum
Do	...do	1 p.m	73	74	24.160	4	..do	....do
Do	...do	2 p.m	71	71	24.130	4	..do	Cir
Do	...do	3 p.m	70	71	24.143	4	..do	....do
Do	...do	4 p.m	71	71	24.143	4	..do	Nimbus
Do	...do	5 p.m	66	68	24.170	4	..do	....do
Do	...do	6 p.m	65	65	24.120	4	..do	Cir. cum
Do	...do	7 p.m		55	24.199	4	..do	Nimbus
Do	Oct. 2	7 a.m	54	54	24.200	1	..do	Nimbus
Do	...do	8 a.m	53	59	24.230	0	Calm	Cir
Do	...do	9 a.m	61	56	24.290	0	..do	....do
Do	...do	10 a.m	58	54	24.189	0	..do	Nimbus
Do	...do	11 a.m	54	56	24.470	0	..do	....do
Do	...do	12 m	54	57	24.191	0	..do	Cum
Do	...do	1 p.m	57	58	24.461	0	..do	....do
Do	...do	2 p.m	59	60	24.461	0	..do	Nimbus
Do	...do	3 p.m	68	61	24.570	0	..do	....do
Do	...do	4 p.m	67	63	24.472	0	..do	Cum
Do	...do	5 p.m	67	65	24.472	0	..do	....do
Do	...do	6 p.m	64	56	24.480	0	..do	....do
Do	...do	7 p.m	58			0	..do	....do

METEOROLOGICAL OBSERVATIONS—Continued.

No. of camp.	Date.	Hour.	Thermometer. Attached.	Thermometer. Detached.	Barometer	Wind. Force.	Wind. Direction.	Clouds.
Alexander's Cañon	1857. Oct. 3	5.40 a.m.	58	61	*Inches.* 24.868	1	West	Cir. cum
Do	....do	6 a.m	61	62	24.996	3	..do	....do
Do	....do	7 a.m	74	64	24.891	4	..do	....do
Do	....do	8 a.m	70	71	24.776	5	..do	....do
Do	....do	9 a.m	71	72	24.899	5	..do	Cir.
Do	....do	10 a.m	70	72	24.872	5	..do	....do
Do	....do	11 a.m	69	70	24.891	5	..do	Cum. stra
Do	....do	12 m	69	70	24.883	5	..do	....do
Do	....do	1 p.m	69	70	24.879	5	..do	....do
Do	....do	2 p.m	75	75	24.862	5	..do	Cir. cum
Do	....do	3 p.m	74.5	76.5	24.866	4	S.W	....do
Do	....do	4 p.m	74	75	24.870	4	..do	
Do	....do	5 p.m	75	75	24.871	4	..do	Cir. cum
Do	....do	6 p.m	69	71	24.960	4	..do	Cir
Do	....do	6.30 p.m	69	70	24.959	4	..do	....do
Do	Oct. 4	7 a.m	50	54	25.000	4	Calm	....do
Do	....do	8 a.m	50	51	24.980	0	..do	....do
Do	...do	9 a.m	60	64	24.970	0	..do	....do
Do	....do	10 a.m	77	76	24.000	3	S.W	....do
Do	....do	11 a.m	75	78	24.000	3	..do	....do
Do	....do	12 m	75	79	24.890	0	Calm	Cir. stra
Do	...do	1 p.m	79	80	24.883	0	..do	....do
Do	....do	2 p.m	81.5	80	24.888	0	..do	....do
Do	....do	3 p.m	87	83	24.870	2	E.S.E	....do
Do	...do	4 p.m	81	79	24.869	2	..do	....do
Do	...do	5 p.m	75	76.5	24.866	2	..do	....do
Do	....do	6 p.m	71	71	24.866	0	Calm	....do
Do	...do	6.30 p.m	70	70	24.866	0	..do	Cum. stra
Do	Oct. 5	7 a.m	51	51	24.870	0	..do	....do
Do	..do	8 a.m	55.5	60	24.870	2	W.N.W	....do
Do	....do	9 a.m	73	74	24.940	2	..do	Cir. cum
Do	....do	10 a.m	75	75	24.903	3	N.W	....do
Do	...do	11 a.m	79.5	78.5	25.000	4	S.W	Cum. stra
Do	...do	12 m	81	81	25.000	4	..do	....do
Do	...do	1 p.m	82	81.5	25.000	4	..do	....do
Do	...do	2 p.m	82	81	24.964	4	..do	....do
Do	...do	3 p.m	85	85	24.680	5	..do	....do
Do	...do	4 p.m	87	88	25.000	4	..do	Cir.
Do	...do	5 p.m	80	79	25.000	4	..do	....do
Do	Oct. 6	7 a.m	65	66	24.872	0	Calm	Cir. stra
Do	....do	9 a.m	72	73.5	24.786	1	S.E	....do
Do	....do	12 m	76.5	74	24.886	2	South	....do
Do	...do	1 p.m	77	77	24.793	2	..do	....do
Do	....do	5 p.m	72	72	24.790	2	..do	....do
Do	Oct. 7	7 a.m	45	46	24.766	0	Calm	....do
Do	....do	8 a.m	55	56	24.766	1	East	....do
Do	....do	9 a.m	59.5	63	24.750	1	..do	....do
Do	....do	10 a.m	63.5	63	24.786	1	..do	....do
Do	....do	11 a.m	65.5	66	24.780	3	..do	....do
Do	....do	12 m	68.5	67	24.778	3	..do	....do
Do	....do	1 p.m	70.5	72	24.756	3	..do	....do
Do	....do	2 p.m	70.5	70.5	24.700	4	..do	....do
Do	...do	3 p.m	70	71	24.690	2	..do	....do
Do	...do	4 p.m	70	69	24.688	2	..do	....do
Do	....do	5 p.m	69	68.5	24.664	2	..do	....do
Do	....do	6 p.m	61	65.5	24.660	2	..do	....do
Do	....do	7 p.m	57	57.5	24.651	2	..do	....do
Do	Oct. 8	7 a.m	47.5	46	24.664	3	West	....do
Station 1	....do	8 a.m	59.5	57	24.877	3	..do	....do
2	....do	9 a.m	79.5	81	25.078	3	..do	....do
3	....do	10 a.m	71.5	73	25.150	3	S.E	Cir
3	....do	12 m	71.5	72	25.170	3	..do	Cir. cum
4	....do	2 p.m	66.5	68	25.354	3	..do	....do
5	....do	3 p.m	68	67	25.486	2	West	....do
6	....do	4 p.m	63.5	62	25.551	3	..do	Cir. cum. stra
Camp 2	....do	7 p.m	60	61.5	25.595	3	..do	....do
2	Oct. 9	7 a.m	45.5	44	25.556	0	Calm	....do
Station 1	....do	9 a.m	56.5	57	25.776	2	West	Cir. stra
2	....do	10 a.m	66.5	68	25.956	2	..do	....do
3	....do	3 p.m	58	58	26.000	4	N.W	....do
4	....do	4 p.m	62	62.5	25.270	4	..do	....do
Camp 5	....do	7 p.m	60	60	26.269	2	..do	....do
Camp	Oct. 10	7 a.m	58.5	57	26.400	0	Calm	Cir. cum
Station 1	....do	8 a.m	59	57	26.450	2	West	....do
2	....do	9 a.m	63	62	26.454	2	..do	....do
3	....do	10 a.m	68	66.5	26.488	1	N.W	Cum. stra

METEOROLOGICAL OBSERVATIONS—Continued.

No. of camp.	Date.	Hour.	Thermometer.		Barometer	Wind.		Clouds.
			Attached.	Detached.		Force.	Direction.	
	1857.		°	°	Inches.			
Station..... 4	Oct. 10	11 a.m...	66	65	26.478	1	N.W....	Cum. stra......
5	....do....	12 m.....	68	68.5	26.472	1	..do.....	....do..........
6	....do....	1 p.m....	71	70	26.456	1	..do.....	....do..........
7	... do....	2 p.m....	70.5	69	26.450	2	..do.....	Cir. cum......
8	....do....	3 p.m .	72	70.5	26.462	2	. do.....	....do........
9	....do....	4 p.m....	70.5	68.5	26.450	2	..do.....	....do........
10	....do....	5 p.m....	68	68	26.388	3	..do.....	Cir.........
Camp.........	....do....	6 p.m....	58.5	56	26.400	3	..do.....	....do....
Do.........	Oct. 11	6 a.m....	43	43.5	26.870	3	S.E.....	....do......
Station..... 1	....do....	9 a.m....	71	70.5	26.800	2	..do.....	....do......
2	....do....	12 m.....	72	70.5	26.800	2	..do.....	....do......
3	....do....	3 p.m....	70	70	26.850	2	..do.....	....do......
Camp.........	....do....	7 p.m....	72	73.5	26.800	0	Calm....	....do.....
Do.........	Oct. 12	7 a.m....	43.5	42	26.850	0	..do.....	Cir. cum......
Station..... 1	....do....	9 a.m....	73.5	71	26.486	2	East.....	....do......
2	....do....	11 a.m...	70.5	68.5	26.666	2	..do.....	....do......
3	....do....	12 m.....	70	71	26.570	2	. do.....	....do......
4	....do....	3 p.m ...	71	68.5	26.528	2	N.E.....	....do... ....
Camp.........	... do....	7 p.m....	68	67	26.580	3	. do.....	....do......
Do.........	Oct. 13	5 30 a.m.	42	40.5	26.700	3	..do.....	Cum. stra......
Station..... 1	....do....	7 a.m....	63	61	26.800	3	..do.....	....do......
2	....do....	9 a.m....	76	75.5	27.150	3	North....	....do......
3	....do....	3 p.m....	81.5	79	27.068	2	..do.....	....do......
4	....do....	4 p.m....	81.5	80	27.200	2	..do....	....do......
Camp.........	....do....	6 p.m....	76	77	27.600	2	..do.....	Cir. cum......
Do.........	....do....	7 p.m....	72	77	27.600	2	..do.....	....do......
Do.........	Oct. 14	6 a.m....	50	48.5	27.684	0	Calm....	....do......
Station..... 1	....do....	7 a.m....	70	72.5	27.888	2	S.E.....	....do......
2	....do....	9 a.m....	71	80	27.764	2	..do.....	....do......
3	....do....	12 m.....	82	69	27.490	0	Calm....	Cum.....
4	....do....	3 p.m....	80.5	82	27.486	0	..do.....	....do......
5	....do....	5 p.m ...	78	79.5	27.258	1	East.....	....do......
Camp.........	... do....	7 p.m....	73.5	74.5	27.280	1	..do.....	....do......
Do.........	Oct. 15	7 a.m....	71.5	70	27.376	2	S.W.....	....do......
Summit of Pass.	....do....	9 a.m....	85	84	26.700	0	Calm....	....do......
Western slope..	....do....	12 m.....	88	86.5	26.900	0	..do.....	....do......
Do.......	....do....	3 p.m....	85	86.5	27.382	1	South ...	....do......
Do.......	....do....	5 p.m....	87	86.5	27.580	1	..do.....	....do......
Do.......	....do....	7 p.m....	69	70.5	27.588	1 to 3	Variable.	....do......
Do.........	Oct. 16	7 a.m....	68	70	27.588	1 to 3	..do.....	....do......
Do.........	....do....	12 m.....	73	72	27.650	1	North....	....do......
Do.........	....do....	3 p.m....	84	82	27.680	2	..do.....	....do......
Do.........	....do....	7 p.m....	68	68	27.700	2	..do.....	Cir. cum......
Do.........	Oct. 17	7 a.m....	70	70	27.950	2	..do.....	....do......
Do.........	....do....	12 m.....	79	77.5	28.130	2	..do.....	Cum. stra......
Do.........	....do....	3 p.m....	82	81	28.340	2	..do.....	....do......
Do.........	....do....	5 p.m....	80	79	28.390	2	..do.....	....do ......
Do.........	....do....	7 p.m ...	72	71	28.530	2	..do.....	Cir. cum. stra..
Do.........	Oct. 18	7 a.m....	59	58	28.790	2	..do.....	....do......
Do.........	....do....	9 a.m....	70	71	28.950	2	..do.....	....do......
Do, ...	....do ...	12 m.....	73	72	29.130	2	..do.....	....do......
Do.......	....do....	3 p.m....	82	81	29.590	2	..do.....	Cum......
Do.......	....do....	5 p.m....	75	74.5	29.610	2	..do.....	Cir. cum......
Do.......	....do ...	7 p.m....	65	65	29.715	2	..do.....	....do......
Do.......	Oct. 19	7 a.m....	57.5	58	29.764	2	..do.....	....do......
Bank of Colorado river....	....do....	9 a.m....	73	72.5	29.810	2	..do.....	Cum. stra......
Do.......	....do .	12 m.....	81.5	81.5	29.850	2	..do.....	....do......
Do.......	....do....	3 p.m....	80	81.5	29.856	2	..do.....	Cir ......
Do.......	....do....	5 p.m....	76	75	29.840	2	..do.....	Cir. cum......
Do.......	....do....	7 p.m....	65	66	29.830	2	..do.....	....do......
Do.......	Oct. 20	7 a.m ...	49.5	48	29.783	3	..do.....	....do......
Do.......	....do. ..	9 a.m...	70	70	29.856	3	..do.....	....do......
Do.......	....do....	3 p.m....	79	76	29.810	3	..do.....	....do......
Do.......	....do....	7 p.m ...	75	76	29.840	3	..do.....	....do......

The foregoing barometrical observations were made with one of "Green's cistern barometers," as both of my "syphon (Buutsala') barometers" were broken before we reached Zuñi, N. M. The observations were principally taken by Messrs. King and Porter, and a few by myself.

Respectfully,

C. E. THORBURN,
Lieutenant United States Navy, and Assistant.

E. F. BEALE,
Superintendent of the wagon road from Fort Defiance to the Colorado river.

Thanks to President Polk and the Mexican War, the United States now stretched all the way from the Atlantic to the Pacific Ocean. The military appropriation bill of 1854 included $30,000.00 "to be expended in the purchase and importation of camels." Ned Beale, at that time, had likely travelled across the country more times than any other frontiersman, although he knew little or nothing about camels. Beale had seen camels during his Naval service in the Mediterranean. The *USS Supply* was dispatched to transport camels from Tunis, Balaklva, Alexandria and finally Smyrna acquiring camels at each port. They departed for the USA with 33 camels onboard. They arrived at Indianola, later Port Lavaca, Texas, arriving with 34 due to a birth. A later voyage acquired another 44 in 1857. They eventually were stabled at Camp Verde, now in the State of Arizona on the Verde River. A visitor's center is on the site.

On April 22 of 1857 the new President James Buchanan notified Beale, then in Washington D.C., "You are hereby appointed superintendent of the wagon road authorized by the last session of Congress, from Fort Defiance to the mouth of the Mojave River." His instructions consisted of three pages from Secretary of War Floyd and his appropriation was $50,000.00 for a working party of not less than twenty-five or more than thirty-five men, a number of strong wagons (to demonstrate the road capable of wagon travel). He was to go to Texas and take delivery of "as many camels as you may deem necessary, not to exceed twenty-five, to test their usefulness, endurance and economy." At Fort Defiance he would be furnished with an escort of twenty-five soldiers plus leadership of one sergeant and two corporals. Beale's estimate of expense included $3,000 for himself, $2,500 for a chief assistant, 17 teamsters and mechanics at $2 a day, and three cooks along with 25 Mexican laborers at $1 per day. In addition, ten wagons and

120 mules at a cost of $15,000 including harness and tack. Also, in that figure were arms and ammo, camping equipment, India rubber boats, bedrolls and presents for Native Americans. His total was $49,462, which begs the question was he working forward or backward? The estimate was approved on April 23rd.

Horses and mules were purchased at New Orleans (having travelled by stern wheeler *Queen* of the West down the Ohio and Mississippi), men were hired at San Antonio, as well as the purchase of a light Ambulance wagon (painted red) which was loaded with surveying instruments, a medicine chest, and a camera and chemicals for developing glass plates.

From New Orleans they proceeded to Indianola, Texas onboard the transport *USS Fashion.*

At Camp Verde, Arizona Territory, Beale presented an order for eight dromedaries and seventeen Bactrians, "to be selected by Mr. Beale himself, with all the accoutrements and men who accompanied them from the Mediterranean." It is noted the "Turks" joined the party at Camp Verde. It should be noted that when the camels arrived in the parties camp, another party member recorded, "Our mules and horses were very much frightened at their approach. They dashed around the corral, snorting in wild alarm." It turned out the mule skinners were more of a problem, alarmed by the camel's "big teeth, unpredictable temper, odor and spitting."

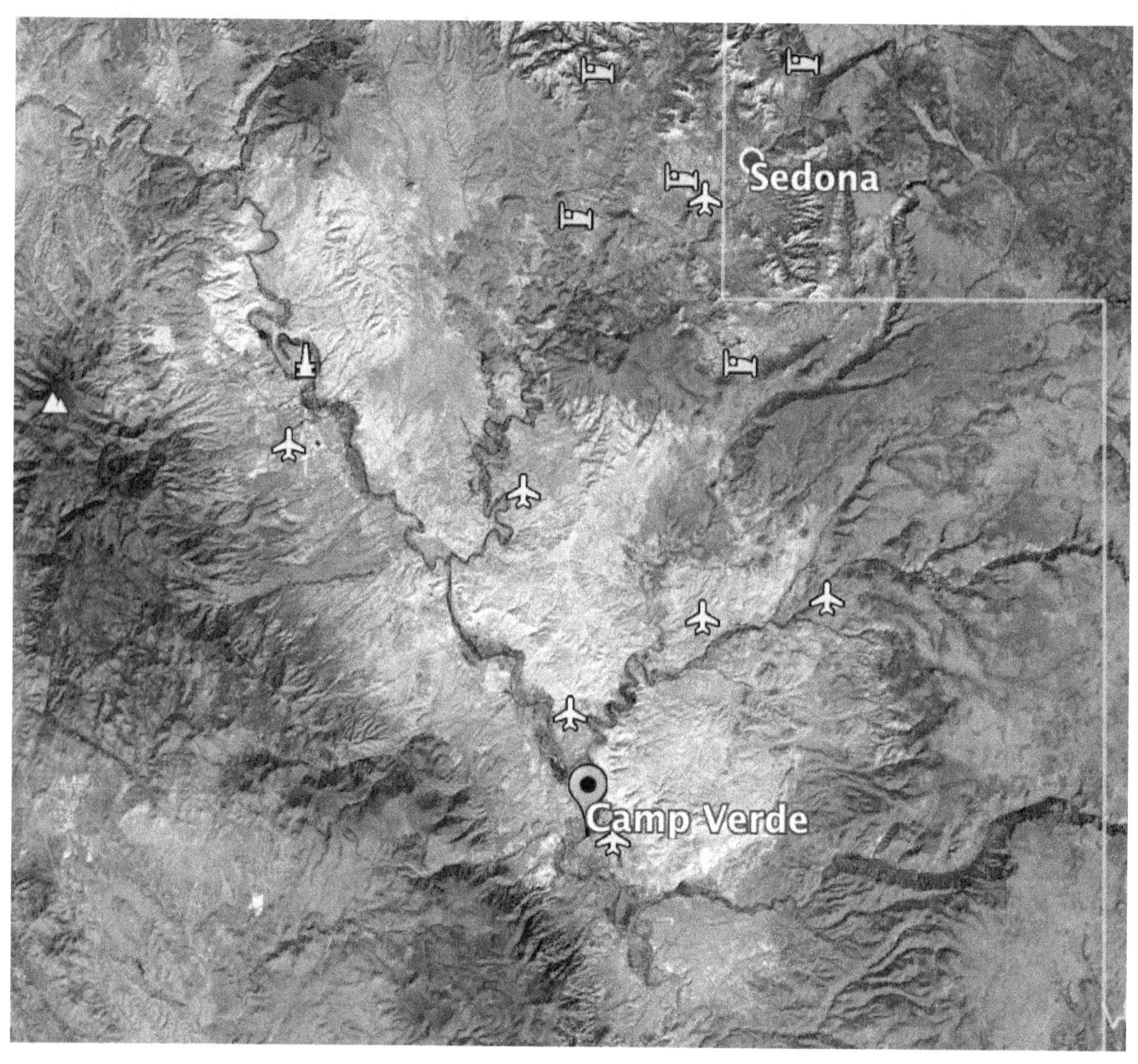

Sedona
Camp Verde

June 25, 1857.—Left San Antonio at 1 p. m., and encamped at the beautiful spring of the San Lucas, having made sixteen miles, the camels carrying, each, including pack saddles, nearly five hundred and seventy-six pounds. This being the first day, and the animals not having performed any service for a long time, they seemed tired on our arrival at camp; but I hope, as we proceed, and they harden in flesh, to find them carrying their burdens more easily. Unfortunately, the only men in America who understand them, and who are thoroughly acquainted with the mode of packing and journeying with them, are some Turks, who came over with them, and who left at San Antonio, refusing to go so long a journey, and alleging that they had been badly treated by the government, not having received the pay due them since January. It seems the appropriation having been exhausted, no one is authorized to pay them, although they left their own country under special contract with officers of the government, and have performed their duties very faithfully. I have placed the camels under the immediate charge of Mr. Breckenridge, jr., assisted by Messrs. Morley and Via.

June 26.—Called up the men at 3 o'clock a. m., and after break-fasting, started at quarter to 5. After travelling a few miles, Mr. Alexander was sent by Mr. Breckenridge to overtake me and report that two of the camels had been taken sick and could not proceed. I sent back a wagon to relieve them of their loads, and hope to have them in camp by sundown. Thus far the camels have not been able to keep up with the wagons, but I trust they will prove better travellers as they become more accustomed to the road. Some of them have not been worked since their arrival, and are, consequently, very soft in flesh. Having travelled nineteen miles through a very pretty country, and through the village of Castroville, we encamped on the Hondo, at 1.30 p m. Water good and abundant, and grass fair.

I met here Mr. McLanahan, of California, who has just returned overland. This gentleman having travelled by both overland routes, northern and southern, prefers very much that of the Central or Cochotope Pass. He followed on my trail, made in 1853, and carried through, with great success, thirteen wagons and a considerable amount of stock.

The camels arrived at 3 o'clock, with the exception of the two sick, which got in shortly afterwards.

Supper over, I went to the stream, which I found to be fine, clear water, in large pools, but not running at this time. The pools were filled with fish, and in a short time my creel was quite full of fine bass, which, in this country, are called trout.

June 27.—Raised camp at 3 a. m., and started at 5. Travelled all day through a beautiful country. The prairies were covered with the most luxuriant grass and flowers. For stock raising or grazing purposes of any kind, the country we have seen to-day is decidedly the finest I have ever met with. Timber quite abundant, and the country sufficiently rolling to relieve it of the usual monotony of flat regions. Post oak and mesquite is the principal growth of timber. The former is useful as food for almost all quadrupeds, especially when the bean is plentiful, which is eaten with the greatest avidity by them, and is

An interesting aside: Not covered in Beale's report, as slavery was certainly a controversial subject in the country, happened on the day of the party's arrival in Indianola. It would not come to light until years later as Beale's papers were being studied. The discovered document was a bill of sale worded: "On June 4, 1857, in Calhoun County, State of Texas, Joseph W. Baldridge, Daniel P. Sparks and Joseph H. Baldridge have this day sold and conveyed to Edward F. Beale our negro man named Jourdan, of copper yellow color, for and in consideration of the sum of $1500, paid by Edward F. Beale, the receipt of which is now acknowledged. The boy, supposed to be from twenty-five to thirty years of age, is healthy, sensible, and a slave."

Beale's family owned slaves. Ned Beale did not approve, in fact had an aversion to the "peculiar institution." He immediately gave Jourdan his manumission papers (freedom). Jourdan became a trusted manservant and stayed at Beale's side for all of Beale's life. One of the many reasons the author has such admiration for Edward Fitzgerald Beale.

Another interesting historical note not covered in Beale's report. While at Indianola Jesse Chisholm was hired as a guide to San Antonio. Chisholm, of course, later named the famous Chisholm cattle trail.

The reference on the opposite page to the value of Mesquite testifies to Beale's long experience as a frontiersman. "The pinole made from it is preferable to that of corn."

very sweet and nutritious.   In the Great Basin, I have frequently eaten bread made by the Indians from this bean, and found it excellent.   The pinole made from it is preferable to that of corn.

Encamped at 1 p. m.   I was anxious to go on four miles further, to the Sabañal, but the camels not being able to keep up, I encamped here on the Comanche creek.   The water, which is only found in mud holes, is bad, and the grass only tolerable.

To-day we have travelled twenty-two and a half miles.

June 28.—Raised camp at 1 a. m., and started before daybreak. Our early start was occasioned by an accident to the guard watch, so that we were called at 1 o'clock, instead of our usual hour, 3.   The first part of our journey to-day carried us through a country very much like that of yesterday.   After travelling five miles we came to the Sabañal, a fine stream of water in large pools, and very clear and sweet.   I fished in it for a short time, but only caught two fine fish. There was abundant evidence that the pools were filled with fish ; but I presume my bait was not sufficiently attractive.

Passing over about fifteen miles, during which distance grass was very abundant, we arrived at the Rio Frio, and found the water not such as the name would indicate, and confined at the crossing to one large pool.   Rising abruptly from the water to the height of about thirty-five or forty feet, and extending for the distance of a quarter of a mile, has a very remarkable rocky bluff, making the otherwise uninteresting appearance of the place quite striking and picturesque. After crossing the Rio Frio, the country seems to change in character very materially—the soil becomes gravelly, the mesquite less abundant, and the grass, though good, not so luxuriant.   Encamped at 12 o'clock, about two miles from the river, there being no grass at the crossing. We find it better to keep our water kegs filled, and camp at a distance from the regular stopping places, on account of the grass.

The distance made to-day is twenty and a half miles.

The camels got into camp at half-past three, some of the most heavily loaded being quite tired.   As soon as they arrive they are turned loose to graze, but appear to prefer to browse on the mesquite bushes and the leaves of a thorny shrub, which grows in this country everywhere, to the finest grass.   They are exceedingly docile, easily managed, and I see, so far, no reason to doubt the success of the experiment.

June 29.—Started at 5 a. m., and found the morning cool, with a fine, fresh breeze blowing.   During the night the appearance of things promised rain, but it ended in clouds and lightning.   We passed through the town of Blacksburg, a straggling village of some dozen inhabitants.   About noon we watered the animals at the Nueces river, which exists here only in one pool of about thirty yards in length and eight or ten feet in width.   The bed of the river indicates that at times it must be of considerable magnitude, though now, with the exception I have mentioned, entirely dry at the crossing.

At 2 p. m. we encamped on Turkey creek, where we found the best water I have seen in Texas.   The country we have passed through to-day is much more rolling than that of any previous day's travel, and the grass equally good.   The road has been excellent all day.

Beale had purchased a 350 pound "Little Giant" corn grinder which proved propitious grinding not only corn but mesquit beans.

Only two "Turks" were convinced to accompany them. Hadji Ali, nicknamed Hi Jolly was actually Turkish, the second, was a Greek, George Caralamba, who forever after was called "Greek George."

Fort Clark, Texas

Brackettville

Fort Clark Museum

© 2020 Google

A detachment of dragoons from Fort Clarke, which has been out on an Indian scout, passed, and encamped near us.

June 30.—Started at 4.45 a. m., and travelled for the first ten miles through fine grass to Elm creek, where we found a very little water in a mud hole. After leaving Elm creek there was no appearance of grass, but the road was very fine. At 11 we arrived, hot and dusty, at the stream of Los Moros, and refreshed ourselves by bathing in the cool, clear waters of the creek. Encamped within a few hundred yards of Fort Clarke, where we were most hospitably received and entertained by the officers. Having replenished our provisions I shall start again in the morning.

Distance made to-day twenty-five miles.

July 1.—I left Fort Clarke at 10, having started the wagons and camels on at 5 a. m. We travelled over a very dry and uninteresting country to the Piedras Puitados, a creek containing some fine pools of water, and well stocked with fish, where we encamped early, the animals having had no grass yesterday. Caught a few fish this evening. The distance made to-day but seven miles. Our whole stock of conversation to-day has been of the genial cordiality with which we were received at Fort Clarke, and the hope we may some day have it in our power to return it.

July 2.—Started at 4.30 a. m., and travelled about five miles, when we stopped to water at a mud hole in the prairie. Three miles further on we came to the Sycamore creek, and found a fine pool of clear water, at which a large flock of wild turkeys were quietly drinking. Our appearance started them quietly on through the brushwood, where Mr. Thorburn followed them, wounding one, which, however, to our disappointment, got off. The country begins to assume a more arid appearance, though the grass is still plentiful, but dry. On our left the mountains of Mexico have been in plain view all day, a relief to the eye after travelling so long on the level plains and broad plateaus over which our road has carried us.

Captain Lee and his wife, who are on their road to his post at Fort Davis, joined us to-day, and we encamped together at a water hole of the San Felipe. This river, like all others we have heretofore met with in Texas, exists at this season, at least, only in holes, sometimes miles apart. We found the water, however, sweet, and tolerably cool

The camels are doing better to-day, and arrived shortly after the wagons. I am very much encouraged to see how eagerly they seek the bushes for food instead of grass, which certainly indicates their ability to subsist much easier than horses and mules in countries where forage is scarce. We encamped at 12.30, and caught some fine fish. Distance made to-day twenty-four miles.

July 3.—Raised camp at 3 a. m., and started at 4. Travelled ten or twelve miles to Devil's river, a clear, broad, and shallow stream of infinite beauty and picturesqueness. The bottom through which it runs, about a quarter of a mile in width, is filled with a fine growth of cotton wood and mesquite. The stream itself is a hundred yards or so in width, three feet in depth, and the bottom of hard rock. On either side the banks are steep, and in many places entirely precipitous, having the appearance of ruins, fortifications, and regular mason

H. Ex. Doc. 124——2

work.   As our line of wagons ascended the hill the camels appeared on the further side, winding down the steep road, and made a picture well worthy the pen of a great artist.   The steep, grey rocks, the beautiful green bottom or meadow, the clear sparkling stream, the loose animals, the wagons and teams, and then old Mahomet, with the long line of his grave and patient followers, winding cautiously, picking step by step their way down the road on the opposite side, was a very interesting and beautiful scene.   We encamped here, and will remain until four in the evening, when we shall water the animals, and go on until ten at night, hoping to reach water again to-morrow at noon ; the distance from Devil's river to the next water being forty miles.   It is at present promising rain, which may give us water on the road.   At 4 o'clock a smart shower of rain relieved the sultriness of the evening, and while still raining we started, (5 o'clock,) and journeyed until eleven, when we encamped for the night.   All were sleepy and tired, and except the sentinels threw themselves on the ground, and were soon fast asleep.

July 4.—Awoke this morning at our usual hour (3 o'clock,) to find it pouring in torrents.   Everything was wet and disagreeable. Blankets were rolled up and thrust into the wagons, and the men cursing their mules with unusual vigor, as if they were the cause of our discomfort; hitched up in the twilight of the morning and prepared for a start.   All day long it rained a cold relentless torrent, accompanied with gusts of wind which drove the chilled water through everything.   Clothing and blankets offered no protection, and the party was soon thoroughly drenched.   No emotions of patriotism availed to warm one against such a storm.   The men sat shivering in dogged silence on their mules, which shivered and humped themselves in return.   It was a terrible fourth of July, and the recollection of the jolly times our fellow-countrymen were enjoying at home made our toilsome and miserable day all the more so.   Occasionally a wagon would stick deep in softened soil, and then more mules had to be hitched to pull it out, ropes hauled on, wheels pried up, and, of course, all this involved the necessity of straightening one's neck, and bending the body from that peculiar curve which is generally adopted in rain storms; so that we had more cursing, and strange oaths, we had not hitherto heard, were brought out in very great force.   Altogether it was a wretched day, and the journey of forty miles without water was made through a deluge.   In the very road itself, there was a stream larger and deeper than any we had seen since leaving San Antonio, except Devil's river.   At last, when near the summit of Dead Man's Pass, and about noon, we broke the pole of a wagon and were brought to a dead halt.   The teams I ordered unhitched and turned loose just where they stood, and some of the men sought what little shelter the wagons afforded, while others, with difficulty, raised a fire with the damp material at hand.   Fortunately at this time (12 o'clock) it ceased raining.   A plentiful supply of coffee, bacon and bread, aided somewhat by a couple of bottles of brandy, which was the remainder of a half dozen presented to me by a friend, the day I left Philadelphia, restored warmth, animation and good humour.   In the course of two hours more, the men went cheerfully to work at mending the road, and repairing the broken wagon. The sun came out in the afternoon, and our camp was soon as cheerful as it had been the reverse. Arms were cleaned and put in order, for we had encamped upon the scene of an Indian massacre, seven whites of a party of nine having been slain here by the Comanches. The camels, much to my surprise, have kept up remarkably well to-day, and have stood the storm better than I thought they would, in fact, apparently as well as the mules. We have made but ten miles to-day, after unremitting labor to man and beast of seven hours.

July 5.—Raised camp at 5 a. m., and travelled eleven miles and a half to the second crossing of Devil's river, where we stopped to breakfast, and turned the animals loose to graze. Our road this morning was, for the most part, rocky, and where it was not was rendered heavy by yesterday's rain. This morning we have rain again, in showers, and a dark leaden sky, which threatens us with another bad day. At 9.30 encamped within a few hundred yards of the river. Grass indifferent.

The camels got in an hour after us.

This morning we found at our camp, for the first time, a shrub, of which we are to see a great deal between this and the end of our journey, and in many places shall find no other wood. It is known as greasewood, and I was delighted to see the camels eagerly seek it, and eat it with the greatest apparent relish. It is certainly very gratifying to find these animals eating, by their own preference, the coarse and bitter herbs, hitherto of no value, which abound always in the most sterile and desolate parts of every road, so far as discovered, which traverses the broad extent of wilderness between the eastern States and our Pacific possessions.

Started at 3, and travelled until 6 p. m.

We passed a military station on Devil's river, but saw none of the officers. It is, I believe, an infantry post, which, of course, is very useful in protecting this portion of the Indian territory; foot soldiers being especially well adapted to the pursuit of tribes always mounted on the best horse flesh to be stolen in Texas and Mexico.

We also passed this evening the scenes of several Indian murders, and the graves of the victims. We followed up the bed of the river, over a very rough road, to Pecan spring, where we encamped for the night.

Distance made to-day twenty-one and a half miles—a very good journey, considering the condition of the roads.

July 5.—We were up last night at 11 o'clock, and the men had already commenced to put the harness on the mules; our wagon-master, Davis, having mistaken the bright moonlight for daybreak. I had not been in bed long when I was told that the men were hitching up, and on sending for Mr. Davis he was made aware, for the first time, of his error, and, greatly to his surprise, informed of the hour. We had gone too far in one thing, however, to correct it—the mules had already been fed their usual morning's allowance of corn, and had eaten it.

At 4 o'clock we started, and travelled until 8.30 a. m., up the valley of the river. The work was very hard on the animals; the rain having made the ground exceedingly heavy, and in many places washed out deep holes and gullies. At 8.30 we encamped at the spring at the head of the river, and shall leave the river this evening entirely.

We have before us another forty mile stretch without water, and shall travel as much as possible of it this evening, and if we find no water in holes on the road, shall make a dry camp, and reach Howard's spring in the morning.

The camels are rapidly improving; they are now becoming accustomed to the road, and getting over the first soreness occasioned by the want of use. To-day they travelled quite as fast as we did, and came into camp nearly at the same time. Encamped this evening at a water hole in the prairie, after travelling all the afternoon in a drizzling rain, which made us quite uncomfortable, though, considering the fact that it gives us water where no other is to be found, we were willing to submit to the little discomfort of sleeping in damp clothes upon the wet ground.

We passed to-day the graves of a party who were killed by Indians last fall. Distance made twenty-five miles.

July 7.—We started at 4.30 a. m., and travelled twelve miles, when we encamped for breakfast. Our crossing place was called Cedar bluffs. The grass is very fine, and water abundant in holes, filled by the late rain. We were passed on the road this morning by the monthly El Paso mail, on its way up, by which I received, forwarded by some of my friends at San Antonio, a box of about two feet square, for which the moderate charge of twenty dollars was made. The dangers of this road, however, justified any price for such matters. Scarcely a mile of it but has its story of Indian murder and plunder; in fact, from El Paso to San Antonio is but one long battle ground—a surprise here, robbery of animals there. Every spring and watering-place has its history or anecdote connected with Indian violence and bloodshed. The country through which we have travelled to-day is entirely destitute of timber, except the mesquite bush, which grows almost everywhere in Texas. The road, though rolling, is excellent.

July 8.—Up at half past two, and off at daybreak without breakfast. We travelled eleven miles to Howard's spring, where we stopped to breakfast and water the animals. This place seems to have been famous for Indian surprises. Near it we passed the graves of seven who had been killed by the savages, and still nearer, within a hundred yards or so, the bones of a sergeant and some two or three dragoons, who were here killed by them. The bodies had, apparently, been disinterred by animals, and the ghastly remains of the poor fellows who had perished there were scattered on the ground. Captain Lee (U. S. army) gave us the history of the fight, which occurred some months ago.

Howard's spring is a small hole containing, apparently, about a quarter of a barrel of water, but in reality inexhaustible. It is directly under a bluff of rock in the bed of a dry creek, and to get at the water it is necessary to descend about eight feet by rude steps cut in the rock; the water has to be passed up in buckets, and the animals

Mesquite

Greasewood

watered from them.   There is but little grass here, and no timber but greasewood and mesquite, and not much of that; a few stunted cedars that grow around the bluff of the spring are neither large enough for shade or fuel.

The rain has brought the grass forward wonderfully, and with it an abundance of beautiful flowers, so that the prairie for the last few days has been filled with perfume and richly colored flowers, which would have been no disgrace to the most costly hothouse.   The whole of the country is vastly improved by these grateful showers, which have clothed it everywhere with verdure, and filled the air with fragrance.

Of large game we have seen but little, but turkeys and partridges abound in great numbers; in fact, the whistle of "Bob White" is with us all the time.

The camels came into camp with us.   We find one great trouble, and the only one, in managing them, is that we know nothing about the method of packing them, and have it all to learn.   In consequence of our want of knowledge in this particular, we have several with sore backs, which, however, I am glad to observe, heal much more rapidly than similar abrasures on the backs of horses or mules.   As soon as we discover one to be getting sore it is immediately freed of its burden, and in a day or two is ready for service again.   They seem almost entirely indifferent to the best grass, and to prefer any kind of bush to it.   To-day we find another food they seem particularly to relish, the name of which we do not know.   The wild grape vine is a great favorite with them, and as it grows plentifully, they will fare well on it.   It seems that they like most the herbs and boughs of bitter bushes, which all other animals reject.   The more I see of them the more interested in them I become, and the more I am convinced of their usefulness.   Their perfect docility and patience under difficulties renders them invaluable, and my only regret at present is that I have not double the number.

After remaining a few hours at Howard's spring we resumed our march, and soon regained the plain.   At the crest of the hill, as we came upon the level land again, we found a new made grave, probably another added to the long list of Indian victims with which the entire trail is filled.

We encamped without water on the open prairie ; grass good, but no timber whatever.

This evening many of our party have seen Indians, but for me, " Ah ! sinner that I am, I was not permitted to witness so glorious a sight."   I encourage the young men, however, in the belief that deer, bushes, &c., which they have mistaken for Indians, are all veritable Comanches, as it makes them watchful on guard at night.

July 9.—Raised camp at 3 a. m., and off before daybreak.   We travelled fifteen miles and encamped two miles from Fort Lancaster, on Live Oak creek.   While at breakfast, some of the officers called and invited us to the post, of which kindness we shall avail ourselves. The camels got off before us this morning, and arrived at camp at the same time.   We are busy to-day repairing their saddles and doctoring their wounded backs, and to effect this purpose I shall go no

Fort Lancaster, Texas, established in 1855, was located on Live Oak Creek one half mile above its junction with the Pecos River. Not occupied after the Civil War.

further, but remain here until to-morrow. Live Oak creek is a clear and beautiful stream of sweet and cool water ; the grass very fine, and wood, (oak, mesquite, and willow,) abundant. Just before descending into the valley of the stream we came to a very steep, rocky hill, overlooking a valley of great beauty and graceful shape. The sides of the hills were covered with the most brilliant verdure and flowers, and our long train, as it wound down the steep descent, and became stretched out on the winding road through the valley, presented a scene of uncommon beauty. It was about sunrise when we arrived at the hill, and the view was so striking that Thorburn and I remained behind to enjoy it until the whole train had passed some distance into the valley.

July 10.—A short time after arriving at camp, yesterday, we received a message from the post informing us of the death of the little son of our travelling companion, Captain Lee, (U. S. A.) This determined us to remain to-day at the post, in order to be present with my men at the funeral. We had all become deeply interested in the fate of the child, which, for the past week, had lingered at the door of death, sometimes giving hopes of recovery, and again relapsing, until all hope was entirely lost. It was buried to-day at 2 o'clock in the afternoon, and our train, which was hitched up and ready for the road, immediately afterwards moved on, and travelled to the Pecos spring, a distance of twelve and a half miles from our previous camp. We crossed the Pecos river eight miles from the fort, and found it a turbid, swift running stream, of about three feet in depth and twenty-ve in width, the water of which is brackish and unpleasant to both. ight and taste.

We were received kindly by the officers at Fort Lancaster, and but for the melancholy occasion of our delay should have passed an agreeable day.

July 11.—Travelled all the day up the valley of the Pecos, which has an average width of about three miles, and is chiefly remarkable for the castellated appearance of the hills on each side. There is no timber, and even the mesquite is smaller than usual, though we find the grass abundant and excellent in quality. The river runs through banks so steep that it was noon before we found a place to water our animals. We encamped then and breakfasted, having made nearly thirteen miles. This afternoon we shall make as much more.

Encamped again this afternoon on the Pecos, having made to-day twenty-four miles. We found the grass only tolerably good, and the water decidedly bad.

The camels are now keeping up easily with the train, and came into camp with the wagons. My fears as to their feet giving out, as I had been led to believe from those who seemed to know, have so far proved entirely unfounded, though the character of the road is exceedingly trying to brutes of any kind. My dogs cannot travel at all upon it, and after going a short distance run to the wagons and beg to be taken in. The camels, on the contrary, have not evinced the slightest distress or soreness ; and this is the more remarkable, as mules or horses, in a very short time, get so sore-footed that shoes are indispensable. The road is very hard and firm, and strewn all

Typical of Beale's sense of humor was an encounter by the trek's geologist, Mr. Williams. While away from camp, breaking rocks for observation, he came upon two Indians. Beale wrote: "The rule in this country, being to shoot at first sight, it was rather an awkward predicament. To the Indians who were as much surprised as the stone breaker, the affair was equally embarrassing. One party armed with musket and revolver, with the memory that the last time he attempted to fire it, it refused to go off. The other party armed with bows and arrows, most probably unstrung as they are normally carried when not expecting immediate use for them. Fortunately there were no seconds on the ground to make the fight imperative. So after regarding each other attentively for a while they started off briskly in opposite directions. And the affair was "thus settled honorably to both parties."

Not so amusing was the entry, "Francisco, teamster, crushed his hand in the wheel."

over it is a fine, sharp, angular, flinty gravel—very small, about the size of a pea—and the least friction causes it to act like a rasp upon the opposing surface. The camel has no shuffle in his gait, but lifts his feet perpendicularly from the ground, and replaces them, without sliding, as a horse or other quadrupeds do. This, together with the coarsely granulated and yielding nature of his foot, which, though very tough, like gutta percha, yields sufficiently without wearing off, enables them to travel continuously in a country where no other bare-footed beast would last a week.

July 12.—Journeyed from 4 to 8½ a. m., and encamped again upon the Pecos, having made nine miles. One of Captain Lee's men went to the river to fish, and soon returned with a cat fish weighing *fifty-seven pounds.* I had it carefully weighed by our own steelyards. This started us all to fishing, but we were not so successful ; in truth, took nothing. We leave the Pecos this evening, and are all glad of it. A more stupid and uninteresting river cannot be imagined—rapid, muddy, brackish, timberless, and hard to get at. We shall go out this evening about fifteen miles and make a dry camp, that is, without water.

Encamped on the prairie. Mr. Williams, geologist, while some distance from camp, and busy in the pursuit of his scientific investigations, came suddenly on two Indians. The rule in this country being to shoot on first sight, it was rather an awkward predicament.

To the Indians, who were as much surprised as the stone-breaker, the affair was equally embarrassing. One party was armed with musket and revolver, with the pleasant remembrance that the last time he attempted to fire it it refused to go off. The other party had bows and arrows. the former most probably unstrung, as they are usually carried when not expecting immediate use for them. Fortunately there were no seconds on the ground to make the fight imperative, so that after regarding each other attentively for a while they started off briskly in different directions, and the affair was thus "settled honorably to both parties." Our horses stampeded twice last night, but did not go far. Grass very indifferent, and no wood. Francisco, teamster, crushed his hand in the wheel.

July 13.—Started at 4 a m. and travelled over an almost level country until we came to the Escondido spring. This water is beautifully clear, though slightly brackish. There is sufficient grass here, but of a coarse innutritious quality. We breakfasted and remained at the spring until noon, when we left for Comanche spring, and travelled over a very fine and level road for eighteen miles. Encamped at Comanche springs, where there was running water about five feet deep, but no timber. We caught some very fine fish. Here the great Comanche trail, on their inroads to Mexico on horse stealing excursions, passes, and thousands of stolen horses have been carried by this road to the Indian country.

July 14.—Raised camp at 4.45 a. m., and travelled ten miles, to Leon spring. Here we found a succession of deep pools of slightly brackish water, but very clear. The road this morning has been excellent, with plenty of grass, but of a coarse quality, and no timber, but a little dwarf mesquite. Our next camp will be a dry one, the nearest water being forty miles distant.   We shall remain here until two or three in the afternoon, and then travel until dark, and camp wherever night overtakes us.   The camels came into camp about an hour after us to-day, not having been packed in time to start with us this morning

Leon spring was supposed by our guide to be five hundred feet deep; everybody said so.   We exploded this popular fallacy by a very simple process, to wit, sounding it.   We found it deep enough to save it from any exaggeration, viz., twenty-five feet.   We started again at 3 p. m., and travelled until 10 at night, when we encamped on the prairie.   At midnight we were awakened by a stampede of all our loose animals, which during the night we had close to the wagons, under a strong guard.   When the stampede first took place I thought but little of it, knowing the animals would not run far, and that the guard would soon bring them back ; but presently, mingling with the sound of the horses' receding footsteps, we heard in rapid succession two shots.   This was startling, as we were in the midst of the Indian country, and it became evident that the Indians had run off our horses. Immediately I ordered all hands called, and taking with me five men, who were quickly mounted on the team animals always kept hitched to the wagons, started out in the darkness to the place where the shots had been fired, and expecting to find some of our horse-guard killed by the Comanches.   We had not gone far, however, before we found our men and the animals, with the exception of six, and discovered that the report of fire-arms we had heard was from the accidental discharge of two barrels of a revolver in the hands of one of our Mexicans.   Much relieved, and with our animals driven before us, we returned to camp and to our blankets.   The stampede has been of service in one respect, it has shown who are willing to fight, and who are not.   Some who have been very loud in the desire to see an Indian skirmish were not as forward last night as I could have desired.   The grass is excellent, but there is no wood.

We have made to-day twenty-eight miles.

July 15.—We raised camp at 3 a. m., and prepared a party to go and follow the trail of the animals which we failed to recover last night.   At daylight, however, by the aid of glasses, we discovered them grazing on the side of the mountain, about four miles off, so that the party prepared to take their trail was spared the trouble of hunting them up.   We encamped at noon at the Hackberry, a mere mud hole, but containing sufficient water for our animals, with tolerable grass, but no timber.   Started again at 11, and having watered on the road at a mud hole, arrived at Barilla spring at about 4. The water at this place is delicious, especially after the brackish stuff we have been drinking.

Our camp this evening is a very pleasant one, on the side of a rugged mountain, and overlooking a green and pretty valley almost shut in by mountains.   It is a great relief, after travelling so long over these monotonous plains to find oneself in the mountains again, and in the region of cool, clear streams and springs.

Distance made to-day twenty miles.

Grass good, but no wood.

From the web: A key post in the defense system of western Texas, Fort Davis played a major role in the history of the Southwest. From 1854 until 1891, troops stationed at the post protected emigrants, freighters, mail coaches, and travelers on the San Antonio-El Paso Road hoping to reach the gold fields of California. Today, Fort Davis is considered one of the best remaining examples of a frontier military post in the American Southwest. It is a vivid reminder of the significant role played by the military in the settlement and development of the western frontier. Named for Secretary of War Jefferson Davis, the fort was first garrisoned by Lieutenant Colonel Washington Seawell and six companies of the Eighth U.S. Infantry. The post was located in a box canyon near Limpia Creek on the eastern side of the Davis Mountains--where wood, water, and grass were plentiful. From 1854 to 1861 , troops of the Eighth Infantry spent much of their time in the field pursuing Comanches, Kiowas, and Apaches.

July 16.—Raised camp at 4, and travelled all the morning through a succession of beautiful valleys, and in the midst of the most enchanting scenery. On both sides of the road the mountain rises to a great height, and is of the most rugged character. On some places, the rock, for miles, is entirely perpendicular for hundreds of yards in height, reminding one very strongly of the palisades along the Hudson; and in others assumes a smooth appearance, but always beautiful. I followed down a chasm, as it seemed, for half a mile, until the rock narrowed to a width of some twenty yards. Here I discovered, to my surprise and delight, a spring of pure and cold water, which found its way through the crevices of the rock, and after running a short distance sank again.

Our camp to-day is near the summit of the Wild Rose Pass, and although the grass is not very good, it is the most pleasant we have had since leaving Fort Clarke.

The camels arrived nearly as soon as we did. It is a subject of constant surprise and remark to all of us, how their feet can possibly stand the character of the road we have been travelling over for the last ten days. It is certainly the hardest road on the feet of barefooted animals I have ever known. As for food, they live on anything, and thrive. Yesterday they drank water for the first time in twenty-six hours, and although the day had been excessively hot they seemed to care but little for it. Mark the difference between them and mules; the same time, in such weather, without water, would set the latter wild, and render them nearly useless, if not entirely break them down.

We started again at 4, and encamped on the Simpia, the stream which runs through the Wild Rose Pass. This evening our ride has been very pleasant, and the scenery still more beautiful than this morning. Oak trees of small growth covered every inch of the mountain not occupied by the solid rock, and the contrast between the gigantic, dark brown rocks, covered with red and grey moss, and the green foliage of the trees, and the still richer green of the cottonwoods and willows which fringed the streamlet on whose bed we are travelling, made a charming character of scenery, and delighted every one in camp.

The road through the pass we found most excellent, and so nearly level that it was impossible, without an examination of the matter, to say which way it inclined.

We have encamped this evening about four miles from Fort Davis, on the spot where two soldiers from the post and the guide were killed, and a drummer boy taken prisoner by the Indians.

The valley is not over a quarter of a mile in width until arriving at our present camp, where it opens to the width of a mile, and the steep palisaded sides of the mountain fall off and give way to an undulating, hilly country, covered everywhere with the finest grass.

Our travelling companions, Captain Lee and his wife, left us here and went on to Fort Davis. To-morrow we shall pass half a day at the post, and then off again for El Paso.

Distance made to-day 23½ miles. Grass rather good, and wood tolerably abundant.

July 17.—Raised camp at sunrise, and went on to Fort Davis, where we were kindly entertained by the officers. Having two wagons to be repaired, I determined to go no further to day.

Distance made about five miles.

July 18.—Employed most of the day at the blacksmith's shop, in driving the repairs of the wagons. In the afternoon we bade adieu to our hospitable friends at the post, and came out about ten miles to Bald Rock spring, where we found excellent water, but no wood or grass. We encamped here for the night.

July 19.—Travelled all the morning through rolling hills, bounded by rocky and palisaded mountains on our left, *and quite near us*, and on the right, but at a great distance, another range apparently of the same character. Everywhere the grass is excellent in the prairie.

At noon we encamped at Bauell springs, where we found a scanty supply of tolerably good water, but no wood.

At 2 we started again, and found a rolling country, and good travelling all the evening to Ojo de las Muertas, (Spring of the Dead.) We passed the grave of a man who had been killed by the Indians, which had the usual pile of stones, to prevent exhumation by the wolves; a shingle at one end, and a sharp stick at the other.

I am convinced water may be found by sinking wells twelve feet, or *less by half*, at Smith's run, which we crossed, and at several other places on the road. The camels are travelling finely. It is worthy of especial note, and I mention it here, while it is fresh in my mind, that since our leaving San Antonio, where my experience commenced with them, I have never seen or heard of one stumbling, or even making a blunder.

July 20.—Raised camp at 4, and travelled until 6 a. m., when we discovered water, about the distance of two miles off the road. It was a mud hole, but served us to water the mules, and was very acceptable, as the nearest *known* water to that at which we encamped last night is thirty-six miles distant. About noon we found another mud hole, a most grateful piece of success, as it saves much suffering, and long marches, without water, with the thermometer at 95°.

We encamped at the mud hole, and shall leave this evening, and go on about ten miles further, and make a dry camp, with the view of breakfasting to-morrow at Van Horn's Wells. Our ride this morning has been utterly destitute of interest. The travelling has been most excellent, generally on elevated plateaus, or across broad and level valleys; but entirely without timber of any description. The grass for the most part good, though a little parched and dry.

We have travelled for the past few days parallel with two ranges of mountains, one on each side of us. They present a barren, rugged and repulsive aspect, and are without timber.

Distance made this morning sixteen and a half miles.

We encamped on the prairie at dark, after making eight miles. We saw two Indians this evening, evidently watching our train, and most likely meditating horse thieving operations against us.

Grass tolerably good; but no wood or water. Whole distance made to-day twenty-four and a half miles.

July 21.—We raised camp at 4 a. m., and travelled nine miles to

Van Horn's Wells—a pool of water of fair quality, but barely sufficient for our animals. I long to reach a good running stream again, where they can drink without struggling and fighting each other for every mouthful. But for this scarcity of water, this country would excel any other in the world for cattle raising. The grass is superabundant, and of most excellent quality, almost everywhere: but the want of a large supply of water is an insurmountable difficulty, and will remain so, until Pope's experiment succeeds.

Our road this morning has been over a country almost level, but not at all interesting. The camels are now being rapidly lightened of their loads, as we have eaten almost all our forage. In consequence, they frequently reach camp before the wagons, and can always do so, if hurried at all. We shall leave our present camp this evening, and go on fifteen miles further, which will bring us near to Eagle springs. To-night we shall make another dry camp, as the drive would be too far for our animals to go on to the next water, without rest.

We encamped for the night on the plains, within ten miles of Eagle spring. Grass excellent; but neither wood nor water.

Distance made to-day twenty-two miles.

July 22.—Raised camp at 5 a. m., and travelled ten miles to Eagle springs. The country is easy for wagons, although our road passes to the right and left of very rough ranges of mountains. The valleys between them, however, are broad and level. I think the average width will be ten miles. The most disagreeable feature is the entire want of wood; the mountains being stupendous masses of rock, entirely destitute of timber and running streams, which we generally associate with mountains, and rendering their appearance forbidding in the extreme.

Our encampment this morning is at the scene of quite a number of Indian devilments. Four men were murdered here by them at one time, and various others at different periods, to say nothing of the numerous bands of cattle, mules, and horses which they have taken from emigrants and others passing here.

The spring rises at the base of Eagle mountain, which is a huge pile of perpendicular cliff, palisaded at the top, and rising gradually without the usual accompaniment of foot hills from the valley. There is quite sufficent water for our animals, and having been eighteen hours without, they are glad enough to get it.

The grass here is very poor, both in quality and in quantity. We started on at 3. The sun was intensely warm, but about 4 a most refreshing shower cooled the atmosphere, and rendered the travelling very agreeable. It was particularly so to us, as we had a journey of thirty-four miles before us, without water. We passed on the road, shortly after leaving the spring, the scene of a battle between the Comanches and some Texas emigrants to California, in which the latter were badly worsted. Travelled some twenty miles, and encamped on the plain without water or grass. To-day we have made thirty miles; a good journey for loaded wagons.

We met two Mexicans on the road whom we supposed to be fleeing from justice. They had probably committed some rascality, and were

San Elizario has an interesting history subsequent to Beale's passing by, a milestone in Texas Ranger lore.

From Wikipedia:

Presidio San Elzeario

In 1789, the site of the old hacienda Tiburcios became the new site where the Spaniards relocated a fort called Presidio de San Elzeario. It had originally been established in 1774, located farther south in the El Paso Valley near the site of modern El Porvenir. It had been moved north to be better able to protect the Camino Real and the towns of to its north Socorro and Ysleta.[6]:46

The town that grew up around the Presidio took its name San Elzeario, or San Elceario (Spanish for Saint Elzear); Saint Elzéar of Sabran is the Roman Catholic patron saint of soldiers. After the Americans acquired the town at the end of the Mexican American War its name was Americanized as San Elizario.[7][8][6]:46–47

San Elizario was El Paso County's original county seat.

In 1877, a conflict, the Salt War, broke out between the town and a troop of Texas Rangers. The Rangers surrendered and two rangers were massacred by the local population. The perpetrators then fled into Mexico and the town lost much of its status.

in a hurry to get out of danger, as according to their story they had ridden nearly eighty miles since day-break.

July 23.—We got an early start this morning, and after travelling a short distance crossed an easy divide, and followed down a cañon leading directly to the Rio Grande. Very soon we came in sight of the green cotton-woods, which mark the line of the river; a most grateful sight to men who had travelled so far without seeing a piece of wood larger than a mesquite bush. The valley of the Rio Grande is here about twenty to twenty-five miles in width, from mountain to mountain, and certainly has no very prepossessing appearance; the mountains on the American side, like those on the Mexican, are destitute of timber, and offer to the eye nought but gloomy masses of rock, where the very spirit of desolation seems to reign. Only the clear fresh green of the cotton-woods in the river bottom creates a point for the eye to rest upon with pleasure; speaking to us, as it did, of a fine stream in which we would bathe our weary limbs; but, like all other anticipations of pleasure, this, too, faded on a nearer approach. We found the river after groping some distance through a dense undergrowth of weeds, briars and willows, a muddy stream about a hundred yards wide; but with such a deposit of mud and quick-sand that even our thirsty mules were obliged to go half a mile below, before we could find a place where we could safely take them to water.

Yesterday our corn being nearly exhausted, I ordered all of the remaining packs to be taken from the camels, in order that their backs might have a chance to recover, where they had become chafed by bad packing. I find they have suffered less than the same number of pack mules would have done on a journey of the same distance. I am convinced that a better and lighter saddle could be easily arranged for them, and shall submit my ideas on this matter fully hereafter. This morning we made twelve and a quarter miles; wood abundant (cotton and willow) and grass enough, but of an inferior quality. We travelled up the valley of the Rio Grande fourteen miles, and encamped for the night. Here I took Mr. Bell and Sandy, and accompanied by Mr. Ford, who had travelled from Fort Davis with us, went on to San Elizario. We travelled until 2 o'clock at night, when we stripped off our saddles, ate a little bread and cheese, and laid down to sleep. After resting two hours, we started again, drowsily saddling our mules in the dim twilight of coming dawn, betook ourselves again with many a yawn to our journey. We travelled on until 11 when we overtook a Mexican train, which gave us breakfast on green peppers and coffee, after which we started once more, and at noon reached San Elizario, hungry and tired. We had ridden, almost without intermission, a distance of ninety-five miles, and had been in the saddle, well nigh constantly, for thirty-six hours.

July 24.—We passed the day pleasantly at the house of Mr. Ford.

July 25.—Still at San Elizario.

July 26.—Our train arrived this morning, and the whole Mexican population, which, since our getting in, had been in a perfectly feverish state of excitement in relation to the camels, had their curiosity gratified. The street was crowded, and when we went on to camp the

Fort Bliss is about as far west as you can get in Texas, very near New Mexico. This from Wikipedia:

On 11 January 1854, Companies B, E, I and K of the 8th Infantry, under the command of Lt. Col. Edmund B. Alexander, established Post of El Paso at Magoffinsville under orders from Secretary of War Jefferson Davis.[20]:23[22] The post was named 'Fort Bliss' on 8 March 1854[20]:23 in honor of Lt. Col. William Wallace Smith Bliss, a veteran of the Mexican War (1846-1848) who was cited for gallantry in action.

There it remained for the next 14 years, serving as a base for troops guarding the area against Apache attacks. Until 1861 most of these troops were units of the 8th Infantry Brigade. At the outbreak of the American Civil War, David E. Twiggs, the Commander of the Department of Texas, ordered the garrison to surrender Fort Bliss to the Confederacy, which Col. Isaac Van Duzen Reeve did on 31 March 1861. Confederate forces consisting of the 2nd Regiment of Texas, under the command of Col. John R. Baylor, took the post on 1 July 1861,[20]:29 and used it as a platform to launch attacks into New Mexico and Arizona in an effort to force the Union garrisons still in these states to surrender. Initially the Confederate Army had success in their attempts to gain control of New Mexico, but following the Battle of Glorieta Pass, Confederate soldiers were forced to retreat. The Confederate garrison abandoned Fort Bliss without a fight the next year when a Federal column of 2,350 men under the command of Colonel James H. Carleton advanced from California.[20]:30 The Californians maintained an irregular garrison at Fort Bliss until 1865, when 5th Infantry units arrived to reestablish the post; these were subsequently relieved by the 25th

Infantry, Buffalo Soldiers, on 12 August 1866, followed by the 35th Infantry two months later.[20]:33, 35

Fort Bliss is still a very active Army base:

From Wikipedia:

Fort Bliss is a United States Army post in New Mexico and Texas, with its headquarters in El Paso, Texas. Named in honor of LTC William Bliss (1815–1853), a mathematics professor who was the son-in-law of President Zachary Taylor, Ft. Bliss has an area of about 1,700 square miles (4,400 km^2); it is the largest installation in FORSCOM (United States Army Forces Command) and second-largest in the Army overall (the largest being the adjacent White Sands Missile Range). The portion of the post located in El Paso County, Texas, is a census-designated place with a population of 8,591 as of the time of the 2010 census. Fort Bliss provides the largest contiguous tract (1,500 sq mi or 3,900 km^2) of restricted airspace[12] in the Continental United States, used for missile and artillery training and testing, and at 992,000 acres boasts the largest maneuver area (ahead of the National Training Center, which has 642,000 acres).] The garrison's land area is accounted at 1.12 million acres, ranging to the boundaries of the Lincoln National Forest and White Sands Missile Range in New Mexico.

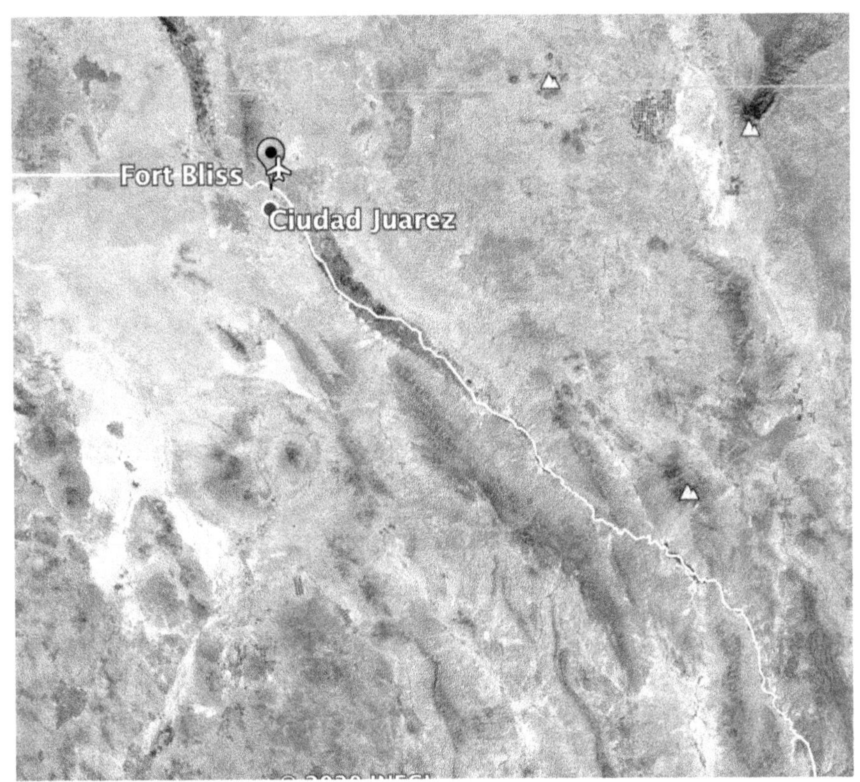

Fort Bliss
Ciudad Juarez

whole town followed. I drove up to Franklin this evening, in order to expedite our departure on the following morning.

July 27.—Spent the day at Fort Bliss, where I was kindly received by the officers. Dined with Mr. McGoffin, and attended a pleasant party at his house afterwards. At 6 in the evening saddled our mules (Thorburn and I) and trotted out to camp—ten miles distant.

Made to-day about eighteen miles.

July 28.—Started before sunrise, and travelled twelve miles, our road following the river to Willow bar. We found the road heavy nearly all the way from recent rains.

Encamped opposite the mountain, about nine miles distant, in which is situated a valuable silver mine, belonging, I believe, to a Mr. Stephenson, who lives near El Paso. It is said the mine is yielding an abundant fortune to its proprietor. It is situated in a mountain on the American side of the river, and apparently of easy access.

The grass at our camp, and also throughout the entire valley, is very plenty, but of a poor quality. Of wood there is abundance of mesquite and cotton-wood, but no other. We have passed to-day numerous herds of sheep, of the small kind common to this country. The wool is coarse and the animal, from the pernicious practice of breeding in and in, small and every way inferior to those of the eastern States.

July 29.—Started by star-light, and travelled about nine miles, when we encamped at a hole of water, about a mile from Fort Fillmore and one and a half from the river. Grass indifferent; mesquite wood abundant, especially a kind of which the camels are particularly fond, the fornia or screw-bean. This bush bears a fruit in bunches, about an inch and a half in length, in the form of a screw. It is very nutritious, and is sometimes used to make pinola by both Indians and Mexicans. The camels seem to like both the branches and fruit better than any other we have met with. Although the branches are covered with sharp thorns, larger and stronger than those which grow on the rose bush, the camel seizes them in his mouth and draws the limb through his teeth, rapidly stripping off the leaves and briars and eating both greedily. Sometimes they bite off branches of considerable size and eat them leisurely, with apparent great ease. Their strength of jaw and teeth seems uncommonly great, greater even than in proportion to their size when compared with other brutes.

This evening was passed pleasantly at Fort Bliss with the officers of the post. We encamped six miles beyond the fort, and only stopped the train long enough to put in forage for our animals. The fort is pleasantly situated, overlooking the river and meadow land lying on either side The ground rises considerably at the post, which is built on the sand hills, and gives it a pretty appearance on approach. At sun-down, we rode on to camp, accompanied by Captain Myers, Major Morris, and my old friend, George Haywood.

It rained slightly almost all night; but not enough to wet our blankets or disturb our sleep.

July 30.—We passed through the towns of Cruces and Doña Ana, where we exhibited the camels to the wondering gaze of the population. Travelled about eighteen and a half miles, and encamped on the river.

Jornada del Muerto, the Journey of death! Ninety miles without water. Thank God, the rain soon came down in torrents.

Here we leave the water, and take the much dreaded "Jornada del Muerto," a stretch of ninety miles without water. We are, however, in hopes that our usual good fortune will attend us, and that the rain will come to our assistance.

This morning our road led us in view of the Organ mountain, about seven miles distant, a most rugged and terribly severe mountain, but containing in its bosom a store of wealth in silver ore which its frowning aspect seems to guard from intrusion; ineffectually, however, as its bowels are being torn and rent by blasting and cutting, in search of the precious contents. This evening we started at 4 o'clock, intending to go out eight miles and make a dry camp; but we had not gone far before it began to drizzle, and soon after the rain came down in torrents. Through the rain we travelled on cheerfully, until a little after dark; cheerfully, for we felt assured of finding rain water in holes on the "Jornada," and for our animals' sake we were willing enough to take the rain.

At night we stopped on the plain, and threw ourselves on the ground, to sleep soundly until the bugle called us in the morning.

After leaving the river, the road ascends about seven miles, which is sandy. At this point the great plain of the "Jornada" is reached, and the road becomes excellent.

July 31.—This morning we started at 4, and travelled until 9.30 a. m. Nothing could exceed the beauty of the country we have travelled over this morning. The whole extent, as far as vision reached ahead, was a level plain, covered thickly with the most luxurious grass, and filled with beautiful wild flowers, while on each side the mountains in the distance, nearly covered with clouds, loomed up grandly. Hundreds and hundreds of thousands of acres, containing the greatest abundance of the finest grass in the world, and the richest soil are here lying vacant, and looked upon by the traveller with dread, because of its want of water.

It is worthy of remark, as a curious coincidence, that at every long stretch without water we have come to, since leaving the Atlantic, we have had abundant rains; all the more remarkable, as the people here say that these are the first rains that have fallen on them for more than a year.

This evening we made ten miles; making, for the day's journey, twenty-four and a-half miles.

Encamped without finding water.

Grass abundant and good; slight rain during the night.

August 1.—Raised camp at 4.30, and sunrise found us some distance on the road. Last night was passed watchfully, Indian signs having been observed. We travelled four miles, and after ascending a short but steep hill encamped at some rain water holes. On the brow of the hill is the grave of two Germans killed by the Indians, from which this place takes its name of the Allemagne. Three miles further on is another place of the same name, where a third German of the same party lost his life. Our journey this morning was short, owing to our finding water and the uncertainty of soon finding it again. The road is excellent and the grass very abundant, wanting only trees and water to make the country perfect. After breakfasting we started again, and, on arriving at the Big Allemagne, found a party of Mexicans journeying to Doña Ana.

In this country the first question is, Indians? And the second, water? Having exchanged views as to the first and most important, we found that, to our sorrow, we should not find water at the Laguna, and that, as no rain had fallen to the northward, we had no hope of any water nearer than the river—fifty miles distant. This at once determined me to spend the day where we were and travel after night. The teams were immediately turned loose and our camp made; the rain water in the holes being abundant.

At sundown we started on our journey again, and travelled till 1 o'clock at night, when we encamped on the plain, having made twenty miles.

The grass is excellent, but the animals, having no water, ate but little.

August 2.—At 4, up and off again. The sun rose hot and fiery, and all betokened a distressing day's journey. Soon we began to see that since the Mexicans had passed rain had fallen upon their trail, and shortly after, to our great joy, a hole containing sufficient rain water for all our animals was found. Camp was made at once, and breakfast. After a hurried meal, the animals being refreshed by water and abundance of grass, we started again and at noon encamped on the Rio Grande. Thus, we have passed the terrible "journey of death," and it has been our good fortune to have had a most agreeable passage of it; rain water as often as we desired, instead of a ninety mile journey without any. The road is already good; the grass, as I have before remarked, everywhere excellent and abundant, and nothing but water required to make it in every way desirable. At present, it lies directly on the road between El Paso and Santa Fé— the dread and terror of travellers, and has cost more loss in the suffering and death of cattle than would pay ten times over for the three wells the government might cause to be dug

The grass on the river bottoms is not good, and we therefore camped on the nearest hills to the river, where we found excellent gramma.

Distance made to-day twenty-five miles.

August 3.—Started somewhat late this morning, (6 o'clock,) and after a short march came in sight of Fort Craig, on the opposite side of the river. I did not cross to it, but from its appearance at a distance of a quarter of a mile it presented a more fort-like outside and aspect than any post we have seen on the road. Travelled up the river sixteen miles and encamped on a hill near it. Grass good, and wood, in the timber of the river bottom, abundant.

The scenery of the river, especially the green meadow and the trees is very pleasant, and to us, who have been so long without the sight of running water, and kept so constantly anxious on the subject of a good square drink, the abundant river is a very grateful object of view.

August 4.—Being anxious to see General Garland, and to arrange matters in relation to the soldiers I am to take with me, I left camp this morning and travelled on ahead as rapidly as the worst road in the known world would permit. At every step our poor beasts sank deep in the sand, and could scarcely lift a leg when we arrived

Again, Beale's sense of humor is demonstrated as he has an exchange with a local, who thought his bright red ambulance a "show wagon."

And again when in Albuquerque and when the "fandangos and other pleasures had rendered them (his men) rather troublesome." And he continued, "I was obliged to apply the oil of boot to administer a copious supply of the oil of boot to several, especially my Turks and Greeks."

at camp. The river bottom, to which we occasionally descended and travelled upon, was filled with corn fields, and tolerably well cultivated after the Mexican fashion, almost the entire day's travel. Herds of sheep, goats, and cattle, sheltered from the scorching sun under the cotton-woods, or standing belly deep in the river, added the grace of pastoral life to the beauty of the landscape.

We passed several towns, and found the fame of the camels had preceded us. At the first, I was taken for the head showman. A crowd soon gathered around us, and a slouchy looking ruffian, acting as interpreter, we had quite an amusing time. Looking at my ambulance, which the taste of the builder had painted a bright red, he commenced:

"Dis show wagon, no?"

I replied, "yes."

"Ah, ha! You be dee showmans, no?"

"Yes, sir."

"What you gottee more on camelos? Gottee any dogs?"

"Yes, monkeys too, and more."

"Whattee more?"

"Horse more."

"Whattee can do horse?"

"Stand on his head, and drink a glass of wine."

"Valgame Dios! What a people these are to have a horse stand on his head, and drink a glass of wine." And we left our friend explaining to his audience what had passed, and filled with admiration for the nation, one of whose humblest individuals possessed a horse capable of standing on his head and drinking wine.

August 10.—ALBUQUERQUE.—Returned from Santa Fé, having aranged all my business with the commanding officer of the deparment. As we were engaging rooms at a wretched fonda, on our arrival here, I was met by Major Rucker, of the army, whom I had known in California years ago. The major kindly offered Thorburn and myself rooms at his house, which we gladly accepted. Business kept me here to-day pretty busy, though I nevertheless enjoyed highly the change from the rough fare of camp to the well supplied table of our kind host.

August 11.—Still in Albuquerque.

August 12.—Started my train on, it being necessary for me to remain until the arrival of the express from Santa Fé. I was anxious, moreover, to get the men out of town as soon as possible, as the fandangos and other pleasures had rendered them rather troublesome. This morning I was obliged to administer a copious supply of the oil of boot to several, especially to my Turks and Greeks, with the camels. The former had not found, even in the positive prohibitions of the prophet, a sufficient reason for temperance, but was as drunk as any Christian in the train, and would have remained behind, but for a style of reason much reserted to by the head of his church, as well as others, in making converts, *i. e.*, a broken head Billy Considine says he has seen a cut glass decanter do good service, when aimed low, but to move a stubborn half-drunken Turk give me a good tough piece of wagon spoke, aimed tolerably *high*.

August 15.—To my delight the express arrived last night, and to-day, at 2 o'clock, we got off.

After travelling some twelve miles or so we encamped on a plain beyond the Puerco.

August 16.—Travelled all day, and overtook the train at the little half Indian town of Covero.

We arrived about sundown, and no one can imagine the pleasant thing it was to us to get back to our flannel shirts, big boots, and greasy buckskins once more. It was home to us.

August 17.—We moved a few miles up the valley and encamped. We are travelling very slowly, awaiting the arrival of Col. Loring, from whom I am to receive my escort, and who is now on his way to Fort Defiance. We are all very impatient, as our work is now about to commence; and whatever fortune is before us, we are anxious to meet it, and have done with all suspense in regard to it. I trust to be in California in sixty days after we once get started.

We find this valley, cultivated by the Indians, in far better condition, as far as crops and prospects are concerned, than any part of New Mexico we have yet seen. They seem to have plenty of corn and wheat, and are, altogether, quite as well off as their Mexican neighbors.

August 18.—Moved camp this morning a few miles up the stream of the Gallo.

Having nothing to do but await impatiently the arrival of Colonel Loring, we only move camp to get better grass. The little valley of the Gallo presents a most singular appearance. Directly down the centre, and rising to a height of some twelve feet, a stream of lava has flowed, and apparently ceased somewhere near our camp of yesterday. This fiery torrent seems to have been nearly a quarter of a mile in width, and looks as if a troubled ocean of molten iron had suddenly cooled. The whole valley is so completely filled with the solid lava as to leave only here and there a narrow belt of meadow; but this is knee deep with the finest and greenest grass, and almost hidden by it, and winding its way through it is the clear, sparkling brook of the Gallo. The stream is quite narrow, in fact no where over six feet in width, but the water clear as crystal and very cool. It is quite deep, being in many places breast high. The contrast with the rough, black, honey-combed rock, which extends as far up the valley as the eye can reach, and the soft velvet green of the little fringe of meadow, is very pleasant, not only to ourselves but to our poor mules, to whom our present short camps seem particularly delightful. On each side of the valley the mountains rise abruptly, and on the left, directly in front, is a palisaded mesa of very considerable height. The term mesa is a Mexican word, signifying table; but out here it is used in reference to mountains. As an English word, when so used, it means a mountain with a flat top, and in this region nearly all are so; in fact, it is an exception to see one otherwise. A sprinkle of rain this evening. Every day for the past ten we have had more or less rain, and at times heavy showers.

August 19.—Still in camp, waiting for Colonel Loring. To-day we made a seine of gunny bags, and caught a large quantity of fish; they

H. Ex. Doc. 124——3

What's often referred to as "cedar" in the west is actually Juniper.

were principally mullet, with a few trout. The stream seems filled with fish, and with a proper net an abundance for any number of men might be taken.

Our camels are doing well here, and seem as fat as when we left, and apparently in better order for the road. On leaving Albuquerque they were packed with an average of seven hundred pounds each; the largest carried nearly a thousand pounds, and the others in proportion to their size and strength. Two Zuñi Indians came into camp this morning and reported Colonel Loring as only a few miles behind, so that we hope to see him this evening. We found the grass on the other side of the creek best, and our mules are now grazing in it belly-deep.

August 20.—This morning I mounted the white dromedary, "Seid," and started back to meet Colonel Loring. The morning was cool and pleasant, and the fine animal travelled off at the rate of eight miles an hour without, apparently, the least effort.

On reaching Covero, some thirteen miles and a half from camp, I found the colonel, who had just arrived, and after a pleasant interview, we started back together; but finding his animals unequal to mine, I rode on to camp again alone, and arrived after an absence of three hours, during which I had ridden twenty-seven miles. "Seid" seemed not the least tired; indeed, it was as much as I could do to hold him on my return, and could not have done so had I not put the chain part of his halter around his lower jaw. The best mule or horse in our camp, in present condition, could not have performed the same journey in twice the time, although they have been fed with corn ever since leaving, and some of the horses not worked at all, having been kept for express duty in the event of accident, while "Seid" has not only worked every day, but been grazed entirely on grass.

I saw some Indians, in the hills at a distance, as I rode along.

I found our men had been fishing again, and had caught, at one haul of our gunny bag net, ninety-six fine fish, which furnished us a good meal for all hands.

There is plenty of wood at this camp—cedar and a few dwarf pines.

August 21.—To-day I sent the camp on to Zuñi, and shall go up with Colonel Loring, whose command reached here last evening, to Fort Defiance, so as to start with my escort from that place. I have determined to take but twenty men, instead of thirty-five, as I do not wish to encumber myself more than is absolutely necessary.

Started at 8 and travelled over a beautifully undulating country for twenty-two miles, when we reached the "Agua Azue," (Blue Water,) and encamped. We found two trains of army wagons here, with their escorts. I cannot imagine why this place should ever have been called "Blue Water." It is a long, ditch-like hole, extending about half a mile, and probably twelve feet in width, by an average depth of two and a half. The water, which, from its name, should be blue, is the deepest colored red brown I ever saw; even more colored than the Pecos, of Texas; differing, however, from that wretched stream in this, that the water is sweet, palatable, and wholesome.

The meadow here embraces, in all, probably two thousand acres of uncommonly fine land, and is covered with a beautiful grass, of a kind

Grama grass, (genus *Bouteloua*), genus of about 50 species of annual or perennial grasses in the family Poaceae. Grama grasses are native mostly to North America, with a few species in Central and South America. The plants are important forage grasses, and several occasionally are grown as ornamentals.

I have not before met with in this country. It grows quite tall, and is very pleasant to the taste and seemingly nutritious; in color a blue green, and very much resembling the blue grass of Jamaica.

There is but little wood immediately at the water, though we found enough drift trash for cooking. A mountain range, which extends all along the road we travelled to-day, and about five or six miles distant, seems to carry good wood in all parts of it. The foot-hills are covered with small cedars, and the higher mountains with large pine trees. On our road to-day a bear crossed our track, just out of gun-shot, ahead of us. Thorburn and I started to cut him off, in some hills to our right, for which he was making, but Bruin outran us, and we gave up the chase, completely out of breath with running.

This evening we have killed a few snipe, which, cooked on a stick, with alternate slices of bacon, have made us a nice supper.

Colonel Loring having turned off the road to a spring, we passed without seeing his command, and shall await his arrival here.

August 22.—The night has been cloudy, with rain, and this morning the sky is still overcast with occasional showers. Fortunately, we have an Indian rubber blanket with us, which protected us both very well, our blankets being spread on the ground close together. Made our breakfast on snipe killed this morning, some black birds, and a piece of mutton we brought from camp with us—a better and a heartier one, and eaten with a more contented mind, than many a one eaten this morning at the best hotel in New York. This morning the colonel joined us, and in the evening we proceed together to Fort De-fiance. Leaving at 2 o'clock, we rode, through a driving rain and heavy mud, but over a very level country, fourteen miles, and en-camped at a muddy spring of sulphurous water, unfit for man or beast. Fortunately, we had filled our canteens at the Agua Azue, and so were provided with good water. Made a pleasant camp in the shelter of a pine grove, but had poor grass for our animals. On our right runs, bounding the valley, a curious range of red sandstone bluffs, some hundred feet perpendicular in height, and stone abutments ex-tending into the plain like capes at sea. This curious formation is said to extend for a hundred and twenty miles to the northward of this. On our left the mountain is covered with fine timber—cedar and pine. The plains are filled with rich gramma grass, which is now hardly long enough to allow our animals to graze on, but which is rapidly springing up everywhere.

August 23.—Yesterday's remarks would apply perfectly, without change, to to-day's travel. We have had the same rain, followed up the same valley, had the same curious range of red sandstone on our right, and finely timbered mountain on our left; the same freshly growing gramma grass; in fact, everything just as yesterday. The valley through which we have travelled is apparently very level, and the road excellent. At noon, having made seventeen miles, we en-camped in a fine grove of pines, just in time to shelter us somewhat from a heavy rain squall.

Started in the afternoon and travelled six miles, and encamped near some rain water. Grass tolerably good. The grass throughout this region is now coming on rapidly, and, once well up, will remain good

The land on which Fort Defiance was eventually established was first noted by the U.S. military when Colonel John Washington stopped there on his return journey from an expedition to Canyon de Chelly.[4] Fort Defiance was established on September 18, 1851, by Col. Edwin V. Sumner to create a military presence in Diné bikéyah (Navajo territory). Sumner broke up the fort at Santa Fe for this purpose, creating the first military post in what is now Arizona.[4] He left Major Electus Backus in charge.[4]

Fort Defiance was built on valuable grazing land that the federal government then prohibited the Navajo from using. As a result, the appropriately named fort experienced intense fighting, culminating in two attacks, one in 1856 and another in 1860. The next year, at the onset of the Civil War, the army abandoned Fort Defiance. Continued Navajo raids in the area led Brigadier General James H. Carleton to send Kit Carson to impose order. The fort was reestablished as **Fort Canby** in 1863 as a base for Carson's operations against the Navajo. General Carleton's "solution" was brutal: thousands of starving Navajo were forced on a Long Walk of 450 miles (720 km) and interned near Fort Sumner, New Mexico, and much of their livestock was destroyed. Following completion of this campaign in 1864 the fort was abandoned once again and it was burned by remaining Navajo, with only its walls remaining. The Navajo Treaty of 1868 allowed those interned to return to a portion of their land, and Fort Defiance was reestablished as an Indian agency that year. In 1870, the first government school for the Navajo was established there.

Fort Defiance

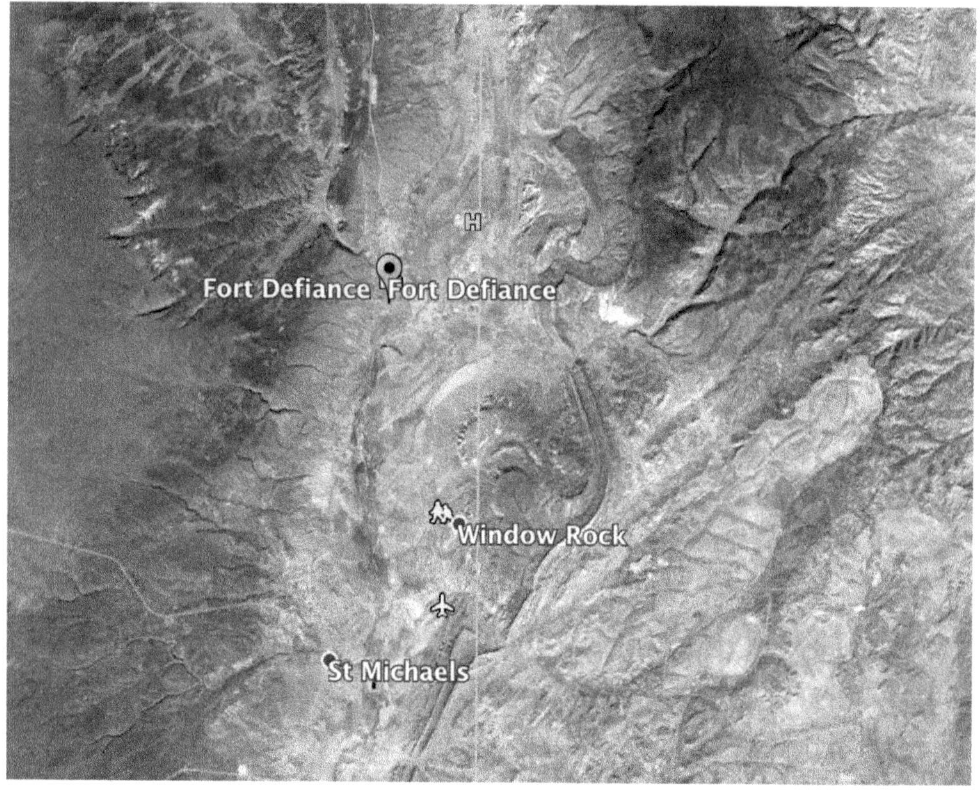

during the winter, and until the first of June. It is nearly all gramma.

August 24.—Started about 7 and travelled nearly eighteen miles, when we encamped on the Puaco, a deep gulley, in which we found water. We are now on the western slope of the Rocky mountains, and the waters from this point all reach the Pacific. Our ascent has been so gradual that no one would have supposed, from the character of the road, we were ascending at all, much less that we were approaching the summit of a most formidable range of mountains. Not even a hill of any size has obstructed the passage of our wagon, and our mules are as fresh after their day's work as though we had been travelling on the great plains. The country through which we are passing is all well timbered with pine and cedar. This evening we found a vein of coal quite near the road where it crosses the Pecos. It seemed to us of excellent quality, and was about two feet in width. It cropped out in two places, and seemed equally large at both. We brought off specimens of it, which we kicked up with our boots from the surface. I subsequently learned that coal in large quantities existed near Fort Defiance and was used at the government shops by the blacksmiths, and found of excellent quality.

Thorburn and I tried our strength this evening in overthrowing a huge rock, which was so perfectly balanced on another that it resembled the rocking stone of the Druids. A very slight exertion caused it to oscillate backwards and forwards like a cradle, though I am sure all of our party could not have lifted half of it. After great exertion, and prizing it with a pine log, we at last overcame its balance and sent the huge mass crashing to the foot of the cliff. This afternoon we came on about ten miles, and finding good grass, wood and water, encamped.

We are now about twenty miles from Fort Defiance, and shall breakfast there to-morrow. Since leaving Albuquerque the weather has been delightfully cool, and at night one finds a pair of blankets hardly enough to keep him comfortable.

Last night the dew was very heavy, amounting almost to rain. This evening mosquitoes are very abundant; but, as the sun goes down, the night is too cold for them to trouble us at all.

August 25.—Started about 6, and after travelling for some hours over a beautiful country, where coal seemed everywhere abundant, we met Captain Carlisle, who was on his way in the ambulance to meet Colonel Loring. As we stood in the warm sun of August, it was most refreshing to see the captain's servant throw off the folds of a blanket from a tub in the bottom of the wagon, and expose several large and glistening blocks of ice, while at the same time the captain produced a delicate flask of "red eye." In ten miles more we reached the post, and were most hospitably received by the officers. Thorburn and myself accepted the invitation of Dr. Irving to live at his house, and are indebted to him for a great deal of hospitality.

August 26.—Rose early, and, with Thorburn and the doctor, took a long walk.

This post is situated at the mouth of a cleft in the mountain, by which the very backbone of the mountain seems to have been cloven down to the level of the plain ; nothing I have ever seen hitherto compares with it. Fancy a great mountain range running in an unbroken line for miles and miles, and here rent asunder, so that a road perfectly level passes directly through what would otherwise present an impassable barrier, and the rock rising in a solid mass, five hundred feet perpendicular, on each side. This cleft is about a hundred yards in width and about three miles in length. Through the centre trickles a scanty stream, which serves to water the gardens of the garrison, which are all made in the cañon, and which seem to be in a most flourishing condition, especially the potatoes. This vegetable is found in this vicinity growing wild. Our walk this morning was constantly through the grandest scenery, and fully repaid us for rising so early.

August 27.—This morning, everything being in readiness, we take leave of our kind and hospitable friends and start upon our journey into the wilderness. No one who has not commanded an expedition of this kind, where everything ahead is dim, uncertain, and unknown, except the dangers, can imagine the anxiety with which I start upon this journey. Not only responsible for the lives of my men, but my reputation and the highest wrought expectations of my friends, and the still more highly wrought expectations of envious enemies—all these dependent on the next sixty days' good or evil fortune. To-day commences it. Let us see what I shall say in this journal, if I live to say anything, on the day of my return here. Left the post at 2 p. m., and travelling over a very pleasant rolling country, reached camp twenty-two miles from the Fork, at a spring called the Collito. On our way we passed the spring called Amarillo, seven miles from the post. The water was the coldest I have ever tasted where no artificial means were resorted to.

At our camp to-night the grass is not good, though wood is plenty—cedar and pine.

August 28.—Raised camp at 5 and travelled until 9 ; country rolling and heavily timbered nearly all the way with pine. Road excellent, but water not to be found. Grass very good in many places. I stopped to rest the men on the Puerco, (the fifth river we have seen of that name,) but found no water in the river. We remained at the Puerco two hours, when we took up our march for this place. Course to-day and yesterday southerly. We found two steep but not high hills on the road this evening, but nothing to make double teaming necessary. Fine timber everywhere—cedar and pine. The road has run, since leaving the spring near the fort, almost entirely through level cañons of sandstone sides, and on the left hand very abrupt and high. The attrition of water has worn them in many places into the most curious and fantastic shapes. Thorburn took a sketch of one this morning, which resembled, on a gigantic scale, an Italian roadside shrine. To-day our journey has been twenty-six miles—course southerly.

We encamped at the Posos, (wells,) a grassy vega of about one hundred and sixty acres, where the water and grass are good and timber abundant—cedar and pine.

Thorburn and I have passed the evening in anxiously examining the very meagre notes of Aubrey, who passed somewhere near where

Zuni Pueblo

Lake Powell
St. George
Page
Farmington
Colorado
Moenkopi Wash
Dinnebito Wash
Polacca Wash
Cottonwood Wash
Grand Canyon
National Park
Cameron
Gallup
Little Colorado
Puerco
Zuni
Flagstaff
Winslow
Holbrook
Zuni Pueblo
Albuquerque
St. Johns
Silver
Creek
Lyman Lake
ARIZONA
NEW
MEXICO
Phoenix
0   25   50   75   100 Miles
N

our trail will go. We have tried hard to reconcile it with the very imperfect maps of the wilderness, but both are so vague that I fear we shall profit nothing by them.

August 29.—Arrived at Zuñi, an old Indian pueblo of curious aspect; it is built on a gentle eminence in the middle of a valley about five miles wide, through which the dry bed of the Zuñi lays. As we approached, cornfields of very considerable extent spread out on all sides, and apparently surrounded the town. This place contains a population of about two thousand souls; the houses, although nearly all have doors on the ground floor, are ascended by ladders, and the roof is more used than any other part. Here all the cooking is done, the idle hours spent, and is the place used for sleeping in summer. Each house or family has a little garden, rarely over thirty feet square, which is surrounded by a wall of mud. Inside of these, and completely encircling the town, are the corals for sheep, asses, and horses, which are always driven up at night. We saw here many Albinos, with very fair skins, white hair, and blue eyes. The Indians raise a great deal of wheat, of a very fine quality, double-headed. The squaws are more expert at carrying things on their heads than our southern negroes. I saw one ascend to the second story of a house by a ladder, with an earthen jar containing a full bucket of water, without touching it with her hands. It was quite amusing to see the men knitting stockings. Imagine Hiawatha at such undignified work. The old Jesuit church is in ruins; but a picture over the altar attracted our attention from the beauty of four small medallion paintings in each corner, which were very beautifully done. After much rubbing off the mud and dust we made out that it was painted by Miguel somebody in 1701. White intercourse (traders) with these Indians seems to have destroyed with them all the respect they had for the Catholic religion, without giving them any in return. Like all Indians who have a fixed abode, they are quiet and inoffensive. A knowledge of this fact induced me to endeavor to establish the same system of old missions in California; but the government did not appreciate the fact as I did, and it has not been carried out. We found here a few indifferent peaches, the only effect of which was to carry us back, in fancy, to home at this season. The melons also were quite poor, almost unfit to eat.

For an account of these people, as they were centuries ago, see Coronado's expedition. For more modern accounts, Whipple's answers every purpose, and is very interesting. Salt, of the finest quality, is found near here by the Indians in the greatest abundance. There is no wood nearer the town than five miles. After leaving camp this morning we had no water until our arrival here. The grass is good, and the wood on the road abundant, until getting within five miles of the place.

Distance made to-day nineteen miles.

August 30.—We spent the morning in arranging a trade with the Indians for corn. The men were all day and until midnight shelling it.

August 31—*Camp No.* 1.—Got off at 11 o'clock, and travelled until 6 in the evening very pleasantly over a rolling country.

As you can see, two Jacob's Well sites show up on Google Earth, but obviously as the explorers are south of the Grand Canyon, the location to the south is the proper one.

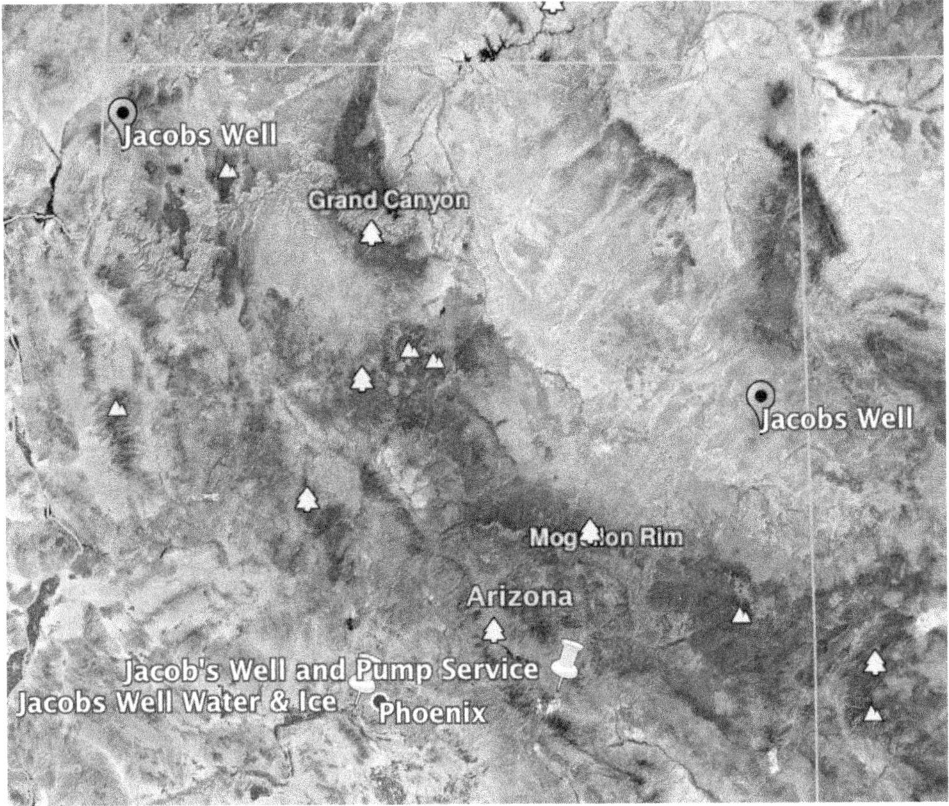

Puerco River (Pig River)

There has been so little rain that there was no water at the usual water holes, two of which we passed. The grass was everywhere of good quality, but the drought had shrivelled it until but little remained. It was all gramma. At 6 we encamped on good grass, but without water. The high rolling prairie, over which we have travelled to-day, has good wood, cedar and pine, and plenty of it everywhere.

September 1—Camp No. 2.—Up at 4 and off at 5 o'clock. We travelled four miles over a level table-land, where the prairie dipped suddenly for a distance of three hundred feet: only about fifty yards was steep, and this our wagons descended without any trouble whatever, other than locking. The perpendicular height of the table-land, over the level of the valley, was about three hundred feet. The valley into which we descended was probably five or six miles in width, and bounded by low hills. Crossing this diagonally, and keeping our good ground and westerly direction, we passed over undulating prairie land, covered with grass for twelve miles, when we arrived at Jacob's Well.

This is decidedly the most wonderful place of the kind we have yet met with. The traveller, following the trail on a level plain, comes suddenly to the brink of a perfectly circular hole of about a quarter of a mile in circumference, and a hundred yards in almost perpendicular descent. The sides of this hole slope very steeply nearly to the bottom, where a basin of apparently very great depth, and about sixty yards in circumference, completed the picture. Around the edges of this pool grow rushes and a few small willows and cedars. The water is agreeable to the taste, though a little brackish, and in it are quite a number of fish. It is only accessible by one trail, which follows the nearly precipitous sides, winding gradually down. Immediately around the well there is no other wood than greasewood, though there are plenty of small cedars at a quarter of a mile distant. I found in the well three blue-winged teal, all of which I killed and found very fat. Our camels, which I packed heavily with corn at Zuñi, (about 750 pounds each,) get along very well, and came into camp this morning a short distance behind the wagons. We saw this morning a fine band of antelopes. Left Jacob's Well at 3.20 p. m., and following a westerly course over a rolling prairie, covered with the finest gramma grass, arrived at Navajo spring, where we found good grass and water. Since leaving Zuñi we have seen, at times, indistinctly, Whipple's trail, and have travelled in its direction most of the time. This evening we struck it just before camping. We have made this evening nearly seven miles, making, for one day's journey, nineteen miles.

To our left, and bearing nearly east, our guide, a Pueblo Indian, pointed out the ruins of an ancient Indian town, which he described as being very curious; but as it was dark when we encamped, I did not visit it. From this place it must be about six miles distant. The cottonwood trees growing near it would be a good guide for any future traveller. At this camp there is no other than greasewood bushes, but within a mile cedar is abundant. Soil, a sandy loam.

September 2—Camp No. 3.—Got up at 4½ a. m., off at 6, and at 8 arrived at the Puerco, but found no water. A little further on, say

Beale's skill as an outdoorsman, frontiersman, is constantly demonstrated, particularly in this dry country. Sighting a copse of cottonwood, nearly always growing near water, following bees and mourning dove, and oft used game trails repeatedly lead the party to water.

Petrified wood (this one 9" in diameter)

a quarter of a mile, found a little rain water in a fork of the Puerco coming from the northwest. The Puerco has a few cottonwood trees on its banks, and at a short distance on the hill-sides, scattering cedars of stinted growth. At 11 we came to the dry bed of the Rio de la Xara, after travelling from our last camp nine miles, over a rolling country, very easy everywhere for our wagons. At the crossing we dug, but found no water; following down the dry bed of the stream for two miles, on the right hand side, is a mass of sandstone rock of considerable size, say half an acre; from this, two hundred yards down, on the left, is more rock, two of which overhang the verge of the bank. Under these, by digging a few inches, we found water sufficient for all our animals, of which we have a hundred and twenty. There is no timber here other than greasewood bushes. The soil is light red clay and sand mixed.

Since leaving Zuñi, the weather has been delightfully cool and pleasant for travelling, and grass good.

Encamped on the Carisso, which is thirteen and a half miles distant from Navajo spring, our last camp. Travelled six miles to the westward, and encamped on a high table-land near the Xara. Grass abundant, but no wood. The country to the northwest is much broken, and very rugged; Sierra Blanca is within sight to the southward, and Moquis to the northwest. The road came up to the banks of the Xara, which we found exceedingly steep, and the whole valley intersected in all directions by ravines, and red clay, mixed with brown sandstone, arroyos, and gullies. Passing a narrow neck of land between the Xara and some very rough country towards the east, we reached a high table-land, covered with beautiful grass, where we encamped; no wood. We found, on the left of our trail, on the table-land, a huge petrifaction, apparently a large tree of probably three feet in diameter.

September 3—Camp No. 4.—Got up this morning at 4, and off at 5½.

It rained on us from the time of our camping last evening until our arrival at this place, Rio de la Xara.

We plodded along this morning through a cold hard rain for a distance of six and a half miles, descending gradually the high table-land on which we had encamped last night. On arriving at the banks of this river, we found no difficulty in getting down without locking a wheel. The country to the west and north, like that of yesterday, was broken and rocky; to the south and east it has softened into a hilly country. Descending in the bed of the stream, the waters of which were discolored and muddy, about a quarter of a mile we found a ravine opening into it, in which was clear water among some cottonwood and much undergrowth, indicating a spring. As one enters this ravine on the right hand side, and nearly opposite the cottonwoods, is a rock thirty feet in height, a part of the brown sandstone cliff, forming the sides of the ravine; and nearly at its base, protruding through the solid rock, and completely surrounded by it, is the butt end of a large petrified tree, the diameter of which is almost three feet; before reaching this, is a detached rock of the same character, through which runs another petrified tree.

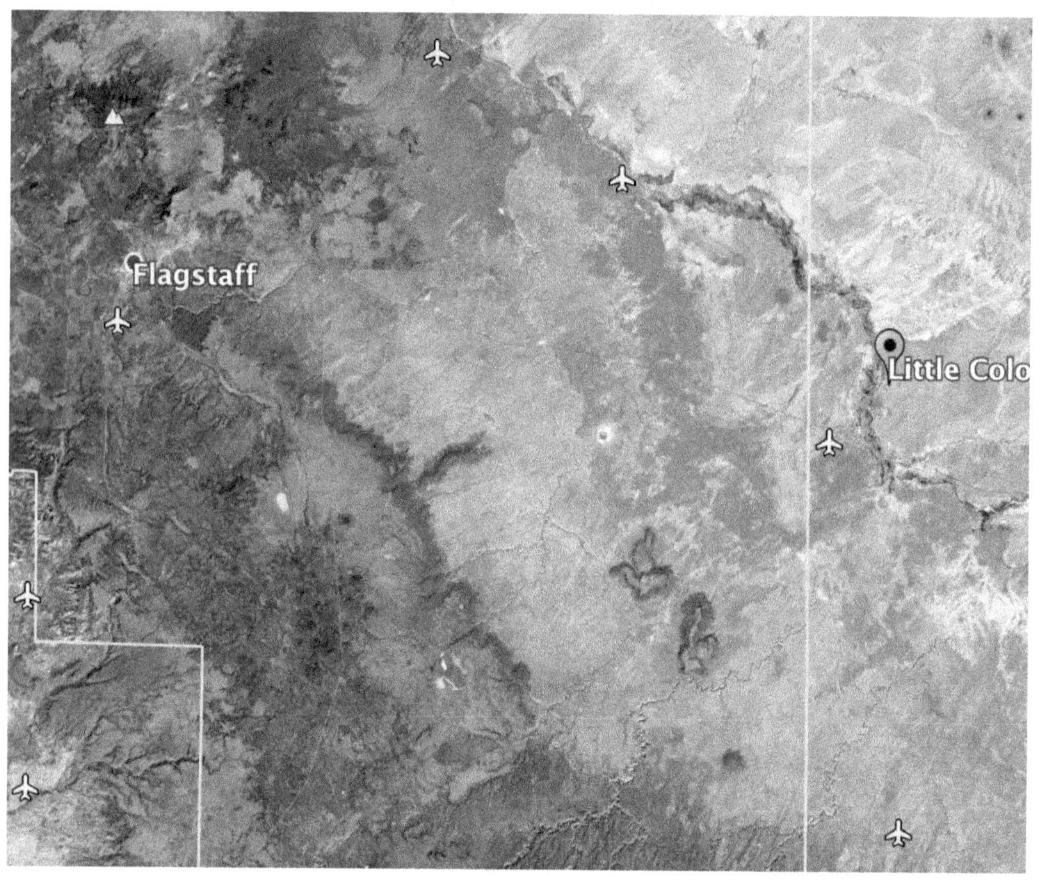

Flagstaff
Little Colo

At 9, we encamped here for breakfast, the grass being good and wood sufficient. Our course to-day has been southwest by south.

Left the Xara at 12, and crossing a low ridge, entered the broad valley of the Pecos. At this point, the valley is about five miles in width, and bounded by low hills on either side. Three or four miles after leaving the Xara, we crossed two sandy beds of streams emptying into the Pecos; but which, I presume, carry no water, excepting in rainy weather.

As we opened the valley, we could see at a considerable distance its point of junction with that of the Little Colorado. Travelling down it, is seen on the left, rising beyond the low hills which bound the valley, the single peak of a mountain, sugar loaf in shape, and looking blue in the distance. It is the most prominent landmark in sight. To the southwest are two conical buttes, which are near the Little Colorado. The soil this evening has been of the same character as that previously noticed—light, sandy loam. There is no wood on the valley, and but now and then a cotton-wood on the banks of the river. The ground is strewn with pieces of petrified wood, and very pretty agates are constantly found.

The weather is still unsettled, and the chances are in favor of our passing another night in the rain, with wet blankets to begin with. It is very cool, and more like our November in the latitude of Virginia, than September. Our course to-day has been a little south of west, and the distance made, fourteen miles. Grass good, and water plentiful.

September 4—Camp No. 5.—We were off this morning at 6 a. m. The pulling was very heavy, owing to the rain of yesterday and last night. Nearly all night it rained on us, and sometimes heavily; but the morning broke bright and clear.

Our road was made this morning down the banks of the Pecos, towards its junction with the Little Colorado. About three miles from our camp, we came to a shallow lake, near the river, where it seemed as though the water might be permanent. The soil is still the same, sand and clay mixed, though clay predominates. Sprinkled over it we found many beautiful stones of various hues and colors, some of which we preserved. Finding the road bad, from the soft character of the soil, we crossed the river for better travelling; but soon after recrossed it where a point of sandstone rock comes down to the banks, and quite near the junction of the two rivers. The Pecos, where we crossed it, contained six inches of water in depth, and about twenty feet in width. Turning the angle of the point of rocks, we came in sight of the cotton-wood trees of the Rio Colorado, at a distance of three or four hundred yards.

The river comes in from the southeast. It was a discolored and shallow stream, some one hundred yards or so from bank to bank; but the water not wider than as many feet, and not over a foot in depth.

The valley of this river is three miles across, and grass plentiful in the bottoms, as well as on the hills, which are quite low. There is abundance of large cotton-wood trees in the bottom, which resembles very nearly the bottom of the Rio Grande. The weather this morning is quite warm, giving us a fine chance to dry our blankets; and

San Francisco Peaks, three summits— Humphreys, Agassiz, and Fremont peaks— on the rim of an eroded extinct volcano 10 miles (16 km) north of Flagstaff on the Colorado Plateau in north-central Arizona, U.S. Humphreys Peak (12,633 feet [3,851 meters]) is the state's highest point, and from it places more than 150 miles (240 km) distant have been seen.

the men are pleased again, after cooking for several days with grease-wood, to see the fine large trees which grow in such abundance here. We have travelled this morning, eight and a half miles, reaching this breakfast camp at 9 o'clock. Our course has been, for the morning, southwest.

The mountain peak to the south, which I mentioned yesterday, I have called Mount Whipple, in honor of the distinguished officer who bears that name.

Left camp at 2.30 and travelled for some distance down the river bottom to a point of rocks which came out from the bluffs towards it, and turning this, we came to and crossed Leroux's fork, which comes in from the northward; the country in that direction looking clean and open.

The stream was quite shallow, not over a half foot in depth, and about fifteen in width. A few cottonwoods lined its bank, and served to mark its course. Proceeding onward in the river bottom, and finding the road heavy with mud, we took a course due west; and ascending a long slope, came suddenly to its termination, from whence we enjoyed a magnificent view. The whole river, for miles, was spread out before us; and far in the distance, over the green tops of the cottonwood trees, San Francisco mountain, rising apparently out of a vast plain, stood as the landmark which was to be our guide for many days. Here we encamped for the night. The country looks open and promises a level road. Should it turn out as much so as that we have passed since leaving Zuñi, we have every reason to congratulate ourselves. The soil over which we have passed this evening, especially that of the hills, is excellent; the grass fully attests that fact. The weather this evening is delightfully cool and clear. Wood is abundant on the river, which is quite near camp. We have travelled a little south of west to day, and made fifteen miles, although the rains have completely saturated the ground, and in many places we have found the road heavy with mud.

September 5—Camp No. 6.—The promise which last evening held out of fair weather has not been fulfilled. It rained shortly after sunset and at intervals during the night. We were off this morning a little after 5. The trail was heavy with mud from the last three days' rain, and yet, although it made our travelling unpleasant, I am pleased to see that the wheels of our heavy and heavily loaded wagons cut in but very little, and most of the time, not more than halfway up the fellies.

Since we struck the river I have observed none of that salt ground, so characteristic of all the streams of this region; and the grass of the river bottom seems of a decidedly better quality, while the low hills which bound the view are everywhere covered with the best gramma grass.

The soil of the bottom is light clay unmixed; and that of the hills, clay of a firmer nature, and mixed with gravel and pebbles, many of which are very pretty.

The view is unchanged since yesterday, San Francisco mountain looking no nearer for the many miles we have plodded towards it.

At 8 we encamped for breakfast near a little fork of the river which comes into this from the north.

The weather is cool and cloudy and threatens more rain. Wood abundant on the river, but none on the hills. We travelled this morning nearly five miles on a course about north northwest, and cut down two arroyos to admit the passage of our wagons. We left our breakfast camp at noon and travelled until 5, crossing over many arroyos draining to the river.

The road was perfectly level, with the exception of the gullies, which we worked down without difficulty. At 4 we passed the ruins of an ancient Indian pueblo. It seemed very old and was scarcely to be traced, except by the broken pieces of pottery which were scattered over the ground. It is a constant source of wonder to us, to see, by the evidences the number of these ruins afford, the dense population this country has once sustained. Scarcely a mile but has its mound of earth and bits of broken pottery ware to mark what was once the abode of a race whose very name has passed away. In those examined this evening we found parts of baked earthen pipes, evidently for the purpose of conducting water, and much of the pottery was prettily figured. The sites of all these places show some eye for beauty of scenery, too; nearly all are placed on gentle eminences overlooking the river and valleys, and not on steep mesas, like those of modern times, and which were built under the influence of fear, after those Bedouins of America, the Apaches, had commenced their ravages over this part of the world. We came eleven miles this evening, making for our day's journey seventeen miles, on a course little north of west.

The soil has been clay, with a little sand; weather pleasant and cool; wood, water, and grass abundant. We passed this evening a large Indian trail going to the north. It seemed about a week old, and we suppose it to be of the Ganoteros, with whom we have been and are at war.

*September 6—Camp No. 7.—*Up at 4 and off at 5 a. m.

It rained on us from sunset until morning; and in consequence of which we found the pulling through the river bottoms unusually heavy and fatiguing to our animals. Our trail was over a perfect level, but the rains had rendered the stiff clay soil of the consistency of tar, so that it stuck to the wheels in large pieces, and to the feet of the mules like snow balls. Add to this the fact that the road was unbroken, there not being even a trail over it, and one may imagine how difficult a job it was to work wagons along. Nevertheless, the soil was not at all boggy, so that with heavy wagons we did not once stall. Passed this morning another large Indian trail going to the northward and crossing our track at right angles.

The weather this morning is bright and clear, but not hot.

We encamped for breakfast near the river, where the grass is excellent and wood abundant.

In sight, a little in advance of us, we see the tops of the cotton-wood trees of Cotton-wood fork, a tributary of the Colorado Chiquito, coming in from the north. Our course this morning has been nearly west. The camels are so quiet and give so little trouble, that sometimes we forget they are with us. Certainly there never was anything so patient and enduring and so little troublesome as this noble animal. They pack their heavy load of corn, of which they never taste a grain; put up with any food offered them without complaint, and are always up with the wagons, and, withal, so perfectly docile and quiet that they are the admiration of the whole camp. At starting there were many, a large majority of the men, who scouted the idea of their going with us, even as far as Fort Davis; but at this time there is not a man in camp who is not delighted with them. They are better to-day than they were when we left Camp Verde with them; especially since our men have learned, by experience, the best mode of packing them.

We have made this morning five miles and a half. The valley of the river bottom here is about six miles wide. On either side the hills slope gradually to the meadow land of the bottom, and, ascending them, extensive plains spread out for great distances, all covered with fine grass.

A spire of the Mogollon mountains and a large blue ridge are seen ahead of us, but at a great distance.

Starting from our breakfast camp at 11, we pulled through the same stiff muddy soil until 1, when the Cotton-wood arrested our further progress. I ascended this stream some distance, and found it running through a wide valley, bounded by plains and low hills as far as the eye could reach. In the direction of the stream, which is northerly, though a great distance off, we saw many isolated peaks, which are said to be in the Moquis country. The stream itself is swollen by rains, and, although now some six feet deep, is doubtless nearly dry when the rains cease.

Finding a good ford over the Colorado Chiquito, and not knowing how soon these constant rains might render it impassable, and, above all, as we would be bound to cross it the next day, I determined to do so at once; so I followed down the Cotton-wood, crossed the Colorado Chiquito, and after going a mile or two down it, encamped near a singular stream coming in from the south. This stream gives no notice of its existence until you arrive directly on its banks, having neither cotton-wood trees nor willows to warn one of its whereabouts. I explored it for some distance up, and found it issuing out of a rocky cañon with precipitous sides. The water is clear, and the immense amount of drift wood, and its character, shows that it comes from a country where cypress and pine of great size abound. Just above, or nearly directly opposite to where we crossed, comes in another stream from the south; but the waters of this are muddy and the banks dotted with cotton wood trees, whereas the waters of the other are clear, showing it to come all its way over a rocky bed.

The climate of this country is exceedingly pleasant, and from the vast quantity of rain that has fallen on us, I should suppose crops might be easily raised without irrigation.

Passed this evening more Indian trails, all going to the northward. Saw much beaver sign, and one fresh dead one, caught by Mr. Coyote last night, and only partly eaten. We saw large fires, Indian signals, in the Mogollon mountains this evening. Grass excellent and most abundant, and for water, the whole river. We have made to-day but

Bull Elk

American Pronghorn Antelope

eleven miles, but, if it does not rain again to-night, shall make up for it to-morrow.

September 7—*Camp No.* 8.—Up at 4, and started at 6 a. m.; but a team having stalled in the river, at the mouth of the little creek mentioned yesterday, it became necessary to take out all the loading. This delayed us until 9, when, after coming three miles, we encamped to breakfast.

We have seen indications of the greatest abundance of game for the past three days. Elk, antelope, and deer, besides beaver and coyotes in large numbers. We leave the river here and take across some low hills, on account of a bend it makes to the northward, and are glad to get to the hills again, where the road will be less monotonous than these flat river bottoms. Wood, water, and grass good, and the weather warm and clear.

Last night we had no rain, though its want was nearly supplied by the heaviest dew I ever saw, and which penetrated our blankets thoroughly. To-the north, yesterday and to-day, we have had the peaks of Rabbit hills in view. They seem conical points, rising to a considerable height above the general level of the low hills and plains around them.

We left camp at noon, and following a stretch of country as level as a billiard table, crossed, after coming five miles, a slight elevation, from which we came into a broad, level and beautiful valley, stretching as far as the eye could reach to the westward and southward. In this valley, the hills of which on both sides are gentle slopes rather than hills, we found a small stream of running water, but very narrow, scarcely over a foot in width. Passing this, we came to a mesa or table-land, the ascent to which occasioned some delay, as it was necessary to cut down the hill before our wagons could go up. Once on the summit, the travelling was again level, until after crossing it, when we came to the abrupt descent of its other side. Here we encamped, having made ten miles, and for our day's journey over twelve. The grass throughout the day has been most abundant, and we have constantly exclaimed, " What a stock country!" I have never seen anything like it; and I predict for this part of New Mexico a larger population, and a more promising one than any she can now boast. The Indians once removed, or kept in check by military posts, this country would be immediately settled with a large population. The river is in sight on our left, well wooded with cottonwood; and as far as one can see, a level country extends to the southward and westward, covered with gramma and bunch grass. Across the river the Rabbit hills look picturesque, but rugged, as, indeed, does all the country in that direction.

The weather this evening has been bright, cool, and pleasant, and the night is cloudless. To-day the soil of the bottoms has been clay, with a little sand; on the mesas it is clay and gravel. For short distances to-day we have had it of a light character, almost like ashes.

We encamped on the top of the mesa to-night, without water, having watered our animals just before ascending it. On the mesas there is only grass wood. In the river bottom, to our right, wood abundant. Our general course to-day has been northwest. We have

The rattlesnake referred to was likely a Mojave Green, small, but very venomous.

seen deer and elk, and the fresh tracks of them are innumerable all over the valley. The valley here, including both sides, is about fifteen miles wide.

September 8—*Camp* 9.—Up at 4, and off at 5.30 a. m.

Descending the mesa, on which we encamped last night, we struck the level valley in a few hundred yards, and our course from that time has been over a succession of level valleys, divided from each other by gentle ridges of very easy grades, generally a mere swell in the prairie. All of them were filled with fine grass, with the exception of bald places, called by the Mexicans playas. These are always of clay, perfectly flat and smooth, and for the most part hard and firm.

At 8 o'clock we found water in two pools, directly on our travelling direction, and without going out of our way to seek it, so that doubtless there are others of the same character.

Shortly after leaving the water, we came, by an inclined plain, to an immense plain or mesa, which seemed to extend over a radius of twenty miles. The soil was firm clay, well packed with gravel, and the whole covered with a luxuriant crop of gramma grass. Travelling in a direct line across this, in a direction nearly northwest, but a little to the westward, we came in sight of the river, but at a considerable distance. The grass was so tempting that I determined to camp here for breakfast.

On these lands, lying at a distance from both river and mountain, there is no timber, so that the traveller must cook with greasewood bushes.

Our trail has led to the west and north for the last day or two ; but 'or no other reason than that a cañon, known as Cañon Diablo—a iere chasm in the plain—prevented the passage of wagons in a due 'est direction. But for this we should now be thirty miles further ,n our journey. It is described by my guide as being a rent in the plain of about a hundred yards across, and with precipitous sides of white rock. This singular chasm extends for thirty or forty miles nearly north and south, which obliges us to go greatly out of our direction in order to pass its mouth. This is the more annoying as the country directly across it presents to the eye almost an uninterrupted plain, rising very gradually to the base of San Francisco mountain and a long spur of the Mogollon range, which comes out to meet the mountain just mentioned. The weather this morning is like a day in the early part of June

We arrived at camp at 9, having made nearly ten miles, on a course a little west of northwest. This morning, on our arrival at breakfast camp, one of our party came near sitting on a rattlesnake, but fortunately it was discovered in time by a messmate, and I despatched it with a wagon whip. It was of the class known as ground rattlesnake, and, although of small size, said to be of the most venemous character.

We left camp at 1, and soon after descended from the mesa to the river bottom. The descent was by a gradual slope. Since leaving the river, we have never been over five miles from it, and the road to it always easy, so that should others, following our trail, not find water where we did, they have only to turn off to the right and make

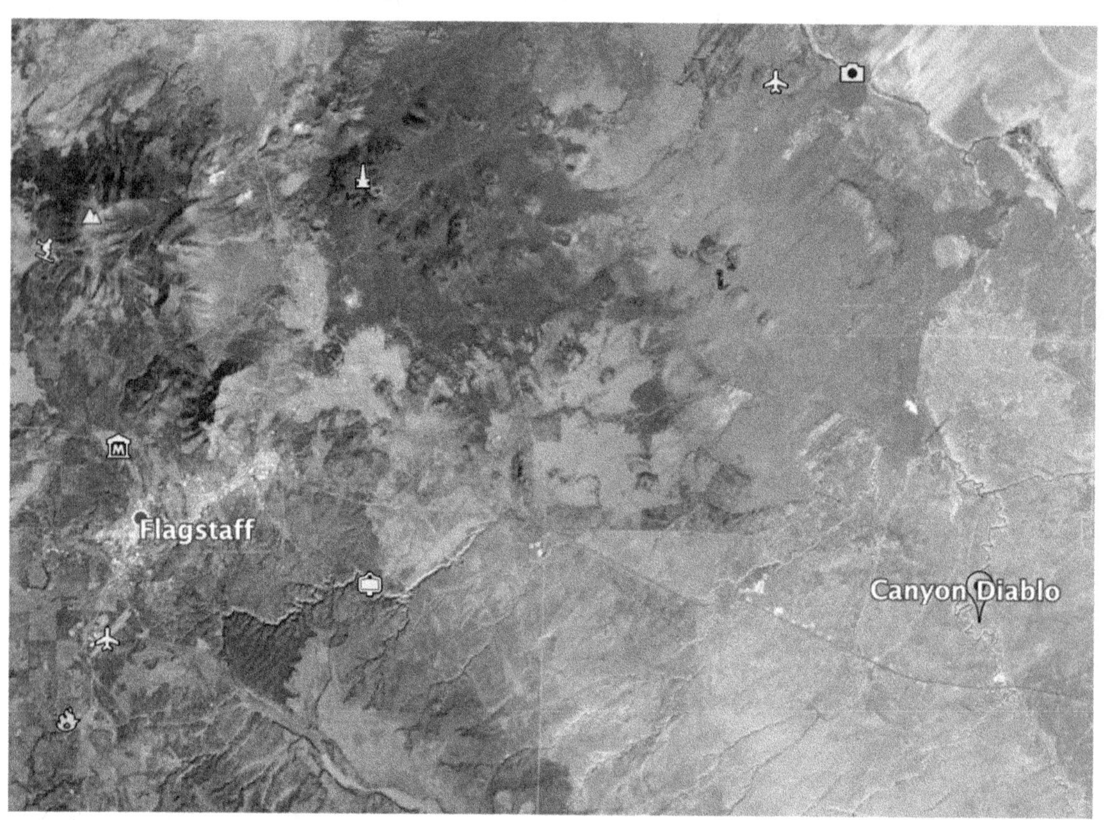

Flagstaff
Canyon Diablo

the river. Travelling down the river bottom, which is here a wide valley on both sides, we came, in ten miles from the previous camp, where we breakfasted, to the mouth of the Cañon Diablo, where we encamped. This point is well marked by four little red sandstone buttes, which rise from the meadow near its mouth, and cannot be mistaken, as they are of peculiar form and isolated in position. They are about thirty or forty feet in height. We are now gaining on San Francisco mountain, which looks down upon us this evening, and to-morrow we cross to encamp near its base. To-day the soil of the table-lands has been the same as that of yesterday. That of the bottom is sand and clay mixed.

The weather this morning is cool and pleasant, and, though clear to us, we see showers falling ahead, and hear the distant roll of thunder.

We arrived at camp this evening at 5.30 p. m., having made nearly twenty miles to-day with our teams. This, over an unbroken road, makes comment unnecessary. Our course has been about west north-west. In yesterday's notes I neglected to mention that up the steep mesa we ascended, and where it was necessary to double teams, the camels packed their heavy loads without the least apparent difficulty, and without a stop, some of them having nearly a thousand pounds, including the cumbersome and heavy saddle. Water, wood and grass abundant.

September 9—*Camp* 10.—Left camp this morning at 5.30, and came three miles. We then encamped for breakfast, as our guide knew nothing of the country in the direction I desired to go, and it was therefore prudent to give the animals water before we started on the road. It was necessary to rest the animals a little, and allow the warm sun to make them thirsty, so that they would drink well before starting, for mules, unless very thirsty, will not drink early in the morning. After breakfast the animals were all sent back to the river, and at 11.30 a. m. we started on a course west by south. After ascending from the Cañon Diablo, we came to a plain of vast extent, and only bounded by San Francisco mountain ahead, and more distant ones to the southward. To the north nothing obstructed the view. This great plain seemed to ascend by a gradual slope to the westward until it met the base of the great mountain of San Francisco. As we travelled over it, we found it occasionally breaking into gentle valleys and small ravines, but all easy and rolling, and between them level floors of extensive table-land ; the whole covered thickly, as far as the eye could reach, with the richest crop of the most luxuriant gramma grass. The entire plain is covered with stones and loose pebbles, and parts of it with small pieces of lava, and occasionally masses of it in rocks, which sometimes reach the altitude of fifteen or twenty feet. Altogether the view, the rich green grass, the distant mountains, and our moving camp wagons, sheep, horses, and camels, made up a beautiful picture. At 3 I sent off three of my men—Stacey, Porter, and Bell—to a line of distant trees, which seemed to promise water, and kept one direction myself with camp. At 4 we came to the banks of a rocky cañon, in which we found abundance of wood and water. Judging from the number of Indians who had evidently made this

I'm sure Beale is referring to cliff dwellings, however I've yet to locate them on his route. These are typical, but located National Monument many miles to the north east.at the Navajo

place a resort, I should think water might be found here at all times. The sides are very precipitous where we found the water, and on going around to the right of the trail, which we went down, I discovered a cave, which had lately been used by Indians as a chamber. The grass on which they had made their beds was still there, as well as a little wood not yet consumed. The chamber is natural and well arched. It would probably shelter twenty-five men quite comfortably.

We came to-day, in all, fifteen miles, on a course west by south, and encamped here at 4 o'clock. The weather this evening is quite cool, and we can see showers falling in the mountains ahead. To-day nothing has impeded our progress but the grass, and this trail, travelled by one large emigrant train, will make as firm and fine a natural road as could be desired.

The creek on which we are encamped is fringed with black walnut of remarkably close texture, and many of them of considerable size. There is also gumpum weed in abundance.

September 10—*Camp* 11.—Up at 4 and off at 5. Following up the creek we came to a curious sort of fortification, or remains of houses. One was of sixteen feet square, and containing but a single room; in another were three rooms, or what had been such. They were of stone, but no lime had been used. All the joints were regularly broken, and the sides, which were over three feet in thickness, were perfectly straight. Only about three or four feet in height remained; the rest had fallen, and lay in fragments at the base.

The morning was cool and fresh, and the night had been quite cold. As the sun rose the temperature became delightful, and has remained so all day. Following the still ascending plain, we approached the mountains, and, crossing a ridge, we came to a table-land from which the view was truly beautiful. Ahead to westward, the whole country was broken into gentle hills and valleys, covered with a heavy growth of noble fine trees, except here and there a mountain meadow of fresh green grass, while to the eastward lay the great plain over which we had so recently passed.

In one of the pleasant mountain valleys we encamped for breakfast; but, unfortunately, it bore no water. Thorburn and I crossed ahead to explore, and found fine, clear water, about a mile from camp, in very much such a place as we discovered it last evening.

The soil to-day has been of clay mixed with decomposed lava; the grass everywhere abundant. We have made this morning eleven miles; our course west, $\frac{1}{2}$ south. We arrived at breakfast camp at 10.30. Game has been seen to-day in abundance—antelope and deer.

This morning we left breakfast camp, and following up the little valley in which we were encamped, turned, after going half a mile, the base of a hill on our left and came around it to the water we had discovered this morning, which, on examination, proved to be the same cañon on which we had encamped last evening, and which was also one of Whipple's camps in 1853.

Cosnurio caves.—These caves are quite extensive, and divided into different apartments by walls. I am quite sure these walls and divisions are not the work of the miserable Indians who at present occasionally make use of them, and who are too lazy and indifferent to

Pines of the size mentioned must have been Ponderosa.

such matters as domestic privacy to make any separate apartments. I think, most probably, this was the work of the race which made the pottery fragments, which are scattered everywhere on the surrounding hills. Certainly it is not of the present tribes, a people differing but little from the root diggers of the great desert and Pah-utes.

One of the escort went off this morning just before we reached breakfast camp, and did not come in before we left. A party was sent to hunt him, but were unsuccessful; therefore I shall camp here this evening, although it was my intention to go twelve miles further, in order that, by building fires and making signals, he may have a chance of being found; but I hardly expect, in fact, I fear he will prove a total loss.

We have made in all to-day nearly fourteen miles on nearly a west course.

The evening is chilly, making camp fires quite pleasant.

On a further examination of the creek I found water in abundance, both above and below where we struck it this morning, and I think quite likely it may be found here at all times. Wood and grass abundant.

Our road this evening lay through a pine forest. A tree I measured of clear pine, and seemingly solid as possible, was five feet in *diameter.*

The soil is the same as this morning, clay covered with decomposed lava. We arrived at camp at 3 o'clock, leaving our former one at 1.30.

We have had an overhauling of the camels this evening; find their backs all doing well, and the animals improving in flesh. The rocks and lava over which we have passed, sharp as it is, have so far had no effect whatever upon their feet.

September 11—*Camp* 12.—Up and off at 5.30 a. m.

The soldier who was missing yesterday has not appeared, although bright fires were kept up all night. It seems hard to determine whether he deserted or went off in a fit of mental aberration. To track him over the rocks would be impossible, and the attempt a useless waste of time.

Leaving our last night's camp, where we had a cold night, and a little frost and ice on the edges of mess kettles, which were left with water in them, we followed up the valley until half a mile brought us to a short hill, ascending which, we came to a glorious forest of lofty pines, through which we have travelled ten miles. The country was beautifully undulating, and although we generally associate the idea of barrenness with the pine regions, it was not so in this instance; every foot being covered with the finest grass, and beautiful broad grassy vales extending in every direction. The forest was perfectly open and unencumbered with brush wood, so that the travelling was excellent.

There has been less of stone to-day, and the soil seems all of rich clay and loam.

Fresh Indian tracks have been seen, probably made last night or yesterday. We came to this breakfast camp at 10 o'clock, having travelled ten miles. Our camp is now at the base of San Francisco

H. Ex. Doc. 124——4

mountain, which looks down frowning upon us. We found no water at this place. Our course this morning has been a little south of west. A shower or two fell on us this morning.

Leaving breakfast camp at 1, we travelled rapidly over a lovely country of open forest and mountain valley, which continually drew exclamations of delight and surprise from every member of the party. Even the stoicism and indifference to beauty of scenery so characteristic of the lower class of Spanish population was moved, and as we passed successive vales and glades, filled with verdant grass knee high to our mules, dotted with flowers, and the edges skirted by gigantic pines, they constantly gave vent to their delight in fervent ejaculations of praise.

After going a few miles, we found it necessary to ascend a mesa, which was rough with stones on the sides, and with flat rock on top. Crossing this, we descended into a pretty valley, where we found some holes of water ; but, these not being sufficient, I sent off a man to explore, and in a quarter of an hour we heard his two shots, which was the signal agreed upon, announcing the discovery of running water. Following the direction, we crossed a low hill, and found the water rising from a marshy place, and running, or rather trickling through high grass, down a short cañon not over a hundred yards in length or more than fifty in width. The sides of this cañon are some ten feet high, and of solid rock, and should this become an emigrant trail, by throwing a dam across the lower end, water sufficient for ten thousand head of cattle may easily be obtained. The expense of this would be but trifling, as the material is all at hand, within twenty steps.

The soil this evening has been rocky on the hills, and clay and black loam in the meadows. We made ten miles this evening, on a course nearly west. San Francisco spring we found nearly dry.

Our camp is under San Francisco mountain, which rears its head far above us into the region of eternal snow. One of its sharp peaks is now covered with snow, looking at that great distance like a white cloud, and is doubtless at all times so. The peak is bare rock, for the vegetation ceases far below it, but from the point where the hardy pine can grow to its base, it is clothed with a noble forest of pine trees.

To-day we saw, besides other game, such as bear, deer, and antelope, some partridges resembling in plumage and habits our own bird at home. They are the first of this species we have seen, all others having been of the blue and gray variety of New Mexico ; and the sight of these familiar birds aroused a momentary pang of homesickness, such as I have not felt for many days. Some elegant squirrels were killed to-day very large and beautifully furred—a silver grey with a rich brown down the back. Scouting close to the mountain I discovered a singular tree. The bark had all the appearance of white oak, while the limbs where cedar. I called the attention of Mr. Williams to it, who has preserved a piece of the bark as well as some of the foliage. Our camp is cheerful to-night, and brilliant with numerous fires. The night being cool, the mule guard and camp guard have built various fires around the spaces guarded, and these, in ad-

Leroux's Spring

dition to the mess fires, give a very pretty effect, especially as each
fire has a dozen logs of the fattest pine upon it.

September 12— *Camp* 13.—Up at 4 a. m.

Being doubtful of the country ahead I sent off Thorburn and five
men to look for water. We unfortunately have no guide, the wretch
I employed at the urgent request and advice of every one in Albuquerque, and at enormous wages, being the most ignorant and irresolute
old ass extant.

This obliges us to do the double duty of road making and exploring,
which is very arduous, besides adding infinitely to my anxiety and
responsibility.

The dew last night was so heavy that on turning out this morning
I at first thought it had rained during the night; on inquiry, however,
I found it had been perfectly clear. The morning air is keen ; but the
sky bright and clear. Thorburn got back at 10, repoting plenty
of water ahead and a good road, so that we shall start immediately.

Leaving our last night's camp, which I called Stacey's spring, after
one of my party, and travelling west by south seven miles, over a
country of the same character as that of yesterday, we came to the
beautiful valley of Leroux's spring, in which I encamped to water and
graze the animals for two hours and a half. The road to the spring,
from our last camp, is rough with loose stones of volcanic origin for
half the way; but the grass as luxuriant throughout as elsewhere.
The timber still retains its large size and abundant quantity. I
measured to-day a pine nineteen feet in circumference and of very
great height.

Leroux's spring is one of transparent sparkling water, and bursts out
of the side of the mountain and runs gurgling down for a quarter of
a mile, where it loses itself in the valley. To reach it we found it
necessary to turn from the course we were steering, and go up
into a little mountain glen from which it flows into the valley.
The soil, though stony on the hills, like that of yesterday, is a rich
loam in the valleys. The day is bright, clear, and warm.

We left our last night's camp at 11, and arrived at Leroux's
spring at 2. We left Leroux's at 4 and a half p. m. and encamped at 7. Our road for the evening lay entirely through a
heavy forest of pine, and was rough with loose stones. The grass,
however, was as good as usual and very abundant. The road was
over a rolling or rather undulating country, and excepting for stones .
would have been excellent.

Our camp, which is in the midst of the forest, and five miles from
Leroux's spring, was soon as brilliant as day with the fires of the rich
pine logs. Our animals having drank heartily, did not feel the want
of water, and we, having brought some with us, found no incon-
venience from it.

September 13—*Camp* 14.—Up at 4, and off at 5.30 a. m.

Emerging from the pine forest, we came upon a rolling country
dotted with isolated hills, and breaking into fine meadow lands, the
borders of which were fringed with a heavy growth of pine and, occasionally, a few oak groves.

Passing to the north of Mount Sitgreaves, and between it and Mount

Kendrick, over a beautiful country, though occasionally stony, we came upon two fine springs, which issue from the north side of Sitgreaves' mountain. The first one I called Porter's spring, after one of my party, and the second Breckenridge, after another.

The weather this morning was quite cold, and last night a white frost covered the ground. We have made this morning eleven miles on a course west eight degrees north, and arrived here at 10.30. Water is very plenty and permanent. Game has been seen in numbers this morning—antelope and deer.

The country seems to open handsomely to the north ; in fact, in that direction it seems a great plain. To the southward Bill Williams' mountain is in sight about twenty-five miles distant. Sitgreaves' mountain about six, due south, and Kendrick's north of east about eight miles. To the west the country looks easy, with valleys and isolated hills, such as we have traversed this morning. The soil this morning has been similar to that of several days past—clay and loam in the valleys, and stony in the mesas and hills. Grass is everywhere good. The appearance of this place is, in the highest sense, sylvan. The fine spring attracts numerous antelopes, which appear and disappear as they glance rapidly through the fine open forest with which it is surrounded, sometimes stopping to gaze at the strangers, and at others racing past at full speed ; and the majestic mountains looking bold and grand, and black with heavy timber, at just a sufficient distance to make the scenery of the amphitheatre in which the springs are one of the loveliest valleys we have seen. This stopping to graze has been fatal to two of the antelope, which have been killed by our party with muskets, directly in sight of the whole camp. The day has been delightfully pleasant since 7 o'clock.

Leaving Breckenridge spring at 2 o'clock, we passed over a rolling country on a west course for some eight miles, when a gradual ascent brought us to a stony mesa of level land over which we journeyed for a mile, when, on arriving at the brink, a great surprise awaited us. Here the most extensive prospect lays spread out before us. Far as the eye could reach, extending to the westward and northward, a wide and level valley of probably thirty miles in width, lead the vision far towards the Colorado, while to the west and south the view lay over a ridge to another valley, seemingly a part or extension of the first, and bounded by a distant range of blue mountains, which I suppose cannot be very far from the great Colorado river. The view was so grand and extensive that we sat on our horses for a long time in silent admiration ; I, on my part, only regretting that we could only go in one direction at one time, so that it was impossible to know and see all the view contained. The soil this evening has been less stony than usual, and the grass, though good, is not as fine as that we have heretofore had.

At 4 we found water in great abundance in a cañon to our right, which was bordered by fine trees. It was a succession of large pools, sufficient for one or two thousand head of animals, and I think, without doubt, permanent wood abundant.

Our general course to-day has been west eight degrees north, and we have made nineteen (19) miles. Could any amount of writing say more for a road? Nineteen miles with mules that have pulled and are pulling heavily loaded wagons eighteen hundred miles; and to-day we have travelled easily, having encamped at the Breckenridge spring for a considerable time. The camels continue undisturbed by the stony character of the country, and can any day go twice as far as the wagons, besides relieving us of all anxiety on their account as to food or water, for they can eat whatever they may chance to get, or do without anything, and drink only when the water happens to be perfectly convenient to camp.

September 14—*Camp* 15.—Up at 4, and off at 5.30 a. m. Travelling six miles over a rolling country in the direction of a wooded butté nearly west from camp, and around the base of which I designed to go; we discovered water about a mile to the right in a ravine, which seems to be a fork of that on which we slept last night. Encamping in a valley among the cedar trees which cover the country here, I sent the animals to the water while the men prepared breakfast. The soil to-day has been clay and coarse volcanic pebbles. The grass (gramma) very good. The temperature of the weather has undergone a very sensible change, being now quite warm althugh cloudy. We encamped 8.30 a. m. As we advance, the country opens handsomely to the westward, and I am now steering for a depression in the mountains due west. I am strongly tempted, however, to alter my course to northwest, for to the northward appears a boundless plain, across whose southern termination our course seems to lead. From an elevation we ascended, I am almost certain a distant mountain to the northward is one at or near the mouth of the river Virgen, and consequently on the other side of the river Colorado. To the southwest is a stack of mountains, one of which is much higher than the surrounding ones, and quite pointed; this I presume to be Picacho.

Our guide has proved so utterly worthless, that I was obliged to send him to the rear yesterday, and only regret that I had not done so sooner. Up to this point he has only served to annoy and mislead me, and it is much better to have no guide, than one in whom you have no confidence, especially as it generally results in your having to do his work for him.

This evening our road, or rather direction to the westward, led us over successive ravines, all leading to the great plain lying to the northward. Intervening, the ground was covered with a thick growth of pine and cedar trees, and apparently this country extended for a considerable distance until it met a rough looking range of mountains, which I suppose is the Aztec range.

A consideration of these facts, and the tempting character of the country to the north and west, determined me to alter my course, and to endeavor to avoid the mountains by striking out upon the open plain. I therefore followed down a ravine into which the train had descended, and at night encamped near the dry bed of a considerable stream, which entered a cañon a short distance below camp. In the morning I shall follow out this ravine, which is filled with fine gramma, to the plain. I called the valley Gramma, from the quantity of that grass which is here found.

September 15—*Camp* 16.—Up at 4, and off at 5.30 a. m.

Following down the ravine for about half a mile, to the point of its entrance into the cañon, we crossed it and soon emerged upon the boundless plain, which stretched, as far as the eye can reach, to the north and west. Here I found the travelling excellent, the soil being of clay and coarse gravel. The grass was not so good though the ground was covered with it; but it was, as yet, young and short. In places, however, it was very good.

The curious appearance of the country to the north induced me to make a detour in that direction, with three of the party (Stacey, Bell and Porter) and Thorburn. Travelling over an apparently level plain, we came suddenly to the bank of a chasm of some one hundred feet in depth, and the same in width. Descending this, on foot, for some distance, I found it to be but the main channel into which many others of the same character, but smaller, emptied.

The sides of this cañon, except in a few places, were perpendicular rock; but the bottom, which was quite level, was filled with fine grass. Crossing this and many others, in search of a point sufficiently elevated to afford a distant view, we spent an hour or two fruitlessly and returned to camp.

Doubtless these cañons all empty the great floods, which the drift wood shows they are subject to at times, into the Colorado or Little Colorado at no very great distance, and I felt the greatest inclination to explore one to its mouth; but as we were uncertain where we should find water for our animals, I dared not do it. Last evening it rained quite a heavy shower, and we are praying for it again this evening. The day has been moderately warm, but cloudy towards noon, and rain has been seen falling some leagues to the west.

These plains are treeless, with the exception of a very few scattered cedars of small growth. We travelled this morning eleven miles on a course nearly northwest, (N. 40° W.)

Breaking up our breakfast camp we followed our northwest course, occasionally bearing more to the westward to avoid the numerous small cañons, all making their way to the great one we had crossed this morning. As we ascended the slight elevations which the almost uniform level afforded, we became more and more impressed with the vast extent of the valley we were following.

On our right, at a distance of probably thirty miles, a long range of precipitous bluffs marked what I take to be the entrance of the Little Colorado into the great river of that name, and most likely at the commencement of the great cañon south of these; and the most prominent landmark in view is a mountain of curious form, rising out of the plain and entirely isolated. The sides of this mountain are quite red about half way up, and the shape of the whole somewhat resembles a bishop's mitre. I called this mountain after Lieutenant Thorburn, of the United States navy, to whose services on this expedition I am greatly indebted. To the southeast are Kendrick, San Francisco, Sitgreaves and Bill Williams' mountains, and to the southwest the peaks of Picacho, while all along to the westward is a line of mesas extending into the plain. To the northwest is a range, but so distant as only to present a dim blue line, and between that and us only a vast plain.

Interesting to note that at the longitude and latitude Beale recorded in his journal that dams could be built where, even in this dry country, there are signs of generous run offs. I searched that location and was not surprised to see a dam backed by a long body of water:

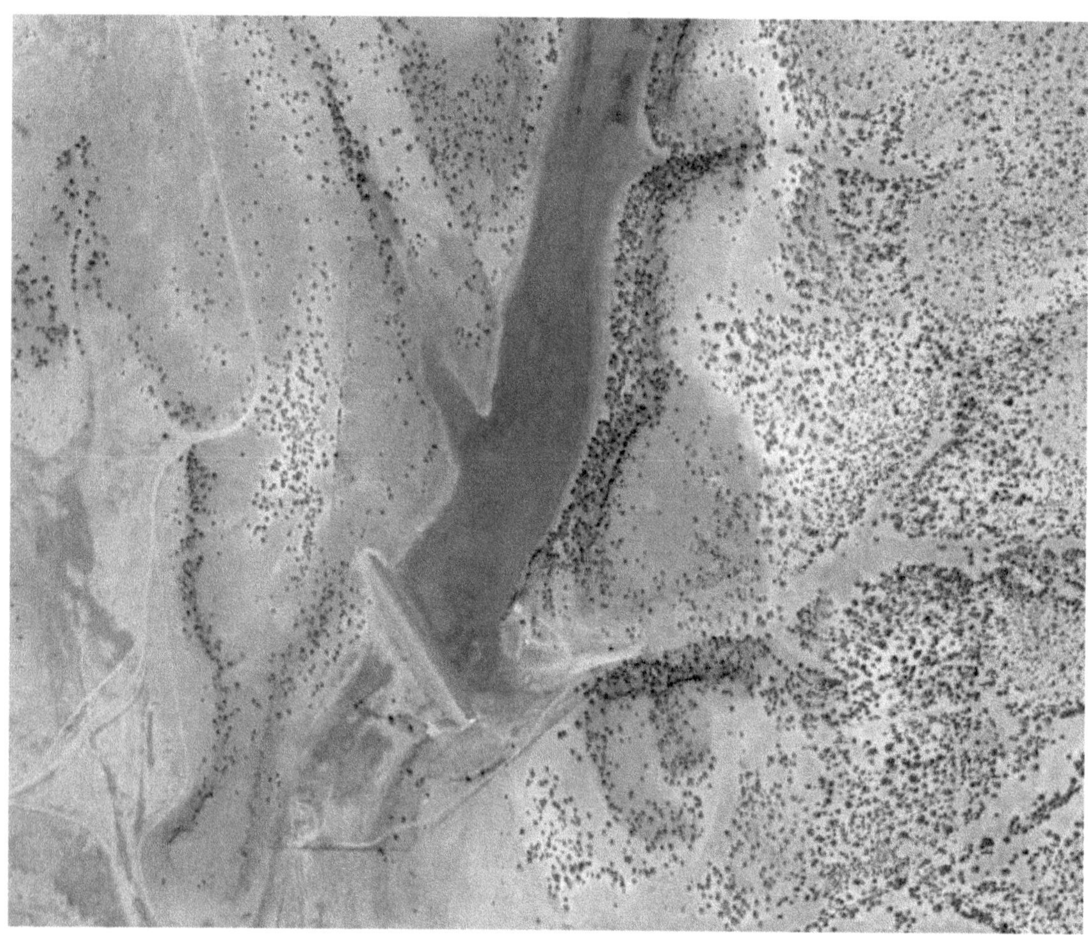

After travelling about eight miles, and water having been found three miles to the eastward of us, we turned off and encamped about sundown, having made ten miles, giving us twenty-one for one day's work. We found the water in one of the cañons already mentioned, a tributary of the large one. It was abundant in quantity and of excellent quality. Large pools of a hundred yards in length were found above and below the place where we struck it, and the green gramma grass covered the sides thickly. Cedar wood was also abundant for camp purposes on the side of the hills. It is worthy of remark that while the grass on the great plain is young and but just sprouting, that near the cañons is well up and in bloom, though I perceive no change in the soil to produce that effect. The soil continues to be clay mixed with the coarse flat angular gravel.

Although it threatened rain yesterday, only a few scattering drops fell, and the evening, though cloudy and cool, was not cold.

On the plain there is but very little growth of wood of any kind ; once in a mile or so one sees a small cedar.

At Albuquerque, before leaving, I found a man who had once passed through with Mr. Aubrey, and, thinking he might be of some use, I employed him. Up to this time he has only justified my expectation by looking out for water, but now he becomes useful as a guide, and, with his assistance, I hope to get along rapidly towards the Colorado. This evening he went off to hunt water before this, at which we are camped, was known to us, and up to this time has not returned, but I suppose he will rejoin us again to-morrow.

September 16—*Camp* 17.—Our man Leco not having yet come in, and it is now noon, I begin to feel a little anxious about him, and shall remain here until he returns, or we can find out what has become of him. Should he not return by night, I shall send a party in search of him, though I can imagine no accident that could happen him, as he is up to all the Indian tricks, and is an old traveller in the mountains and plains. At 4 p. m. I sent out a party of three men to look him up, with orders to search until to-morrow night, and then return ; or, if they should find any Indian village sooner, so as to make it certain he had been slain by them, to come in immediately, so that we might make up a party to surround them and take due vengeance.

The weather to-day cold and windy.

September 17—*Camp* 17.—No news yet of Leco or the party sent in search of him. Finding being in camp tiresome, Thorburn and I walked some miles down the creek towards its entrance into the Colorado. We found water every hundred yards or so, and I am confident it may be relied on as permanent. The pools were large, some of them over a hundred yards in extent, and from one to three feet in depth. I am led to the belief in the permanence of this water from the fact that we found and killed here, at our camp, snipe, ducks, and crane ; and that the water extends all the way to the river in pools is equally certain, otherwise the antelope would have made this place their resort for water, and abundance of sign would be found here, which is not the case, although they abound on the plains all around. The Indians, too, if this were the only water,

Bunch Grass

would have a rancheria here, of which we should see the remains. The grass is equal to any we have found on the road, and is gramma mixed with bunch grass.

The soil is the same as that heretofore described in this region.

We find the whole country to the eastward cut up in cañons, all leading, I suppose, to the little Colorado, which is marked by the cliffs in sight of our camp, and is probably some thirty miles to the north of us.

To-day the weather is pleasantly warm, with a brisk southwest wind blowing and a few clouds.

Leaving this camp I shall endeavor to find a road due west to the Colorado, which, although here running east and west, takes a bend a hundred miles to the westward, and runs nearly north and south.

Towards sunset the party sent in search of the missing guide returned with him. It appears that in getting off to light a fire his mule had escaped, and knowing it to be one of the most valuable in our mulada, he had followed it all the remainder of the evening and the whole of the next night, only catching it, sometime in the forenoon of the next day, and then supposing camp had held the direction it was going when he left it, and not being aware of our finding water here, he had kept on until overtaken by the men sent in search of him. He had been forty-eight hours without water or food, and must doubtless have perished had he not been found.

September 18—*Camp* 17.—The morning is bright, clear and warm. We have killed, this morning, at the water here, blue-winged teal and other ducks, flocks of which are flying and alighting around the pools, and the English snipe, the first of that species we have met with about here.

All signs indicate this as permanent water, and its very great abundance makes the discovery a most valuable one to this road. Water may be had, however, in any quantity every five miles from the Colorado Chiquito or Zuñi to the river, by the expenditure of a few thousand dollars by the government in building dams across aroyos and cañons, which the rain would fill every month. A dam here, for instance, is not probably needed; but if it were, the stone and other material is ready cut by nature, and only wants the hand of man to place it in position to confine millions and millions of gallons. These cañons are from a hundred to two hundred feet in depth; at times a chasm with precipitous sides; at others only precipitous on one side; and all of them show, by drift wood and other unmistakeable signs, that they are *frequently* bold running streams. One can see, therefore, how simple a matter it would be to make the dams and to insure a bountiful supply of water at all seasons, should this, contrary to all signs, prove not to be permanent.

These remarks apply equally to all other parts of the road from Zuñi, and I cannot but think that money expended on a certainty of this kind would be spent to better purpose than in the uncertain process of artesian wells.

We leave here to-day at noon to explore this great plain, and shall endeavor to go as nearly west as possible to the Colorado Grande. Leaving King's creek, so called after one of my party, at noon, we travelled until 4, over an undulating plain, which stretched out to the northward and westward. I should suppose this plain to be, at its widest part, from eighty to one hundred miles in width. Its soil is light, loose yellow clay and coarse gravel, and is without trees, bearing only greasewood bushes for fuel.

To our left, that is, to the south and southwest, a range of mountains seems to terminate in long cape-like mesas, which extend into the plain we are traversing. Ahead the view is unbounded, only the blue points of a mountain appearing far in the distance. The bluffs of what we take to be the Little Colorado, and Thorburn's mountain to the east, are the most prominent objects in sight. The grass at our camp is short, but green and fresh, and has been so since leaving King's creek. The weather is clear and warm, making the uncertainty of water ahead rather unpleasant. However, by travelling to-night and part of to-morrow I hope we shall find it.

We have made this evening twelve miles, and shall go on again at sundown, and travel until midnight.

The slopes of the mesas on our left seem to be covered with a heavy growth of pine timber. The nearest is about ten miles south of us. Leaving our supper camp at dark, we travelled by night, and the night dark, for ten miles across the country to the northwest, and so level was the surface, that not a wagon stopped for a moment. At 10 we halted and encamped for the night. Going ahead with two or three of my party, I made fires every three or four miles, as guides to the wagons, and such was the level character of the country, that those behind told me they could frequently see the flash of my match as I would light it to kindle the fire. In gathering greasewood bushes for one of the fires, Thorburn picked up in his hand a rattlesnake, but fortunately the night was so cool that, I presume, the reptile was torpid with cold, so then when the fire blazed up I shot him with my pistol where Thorburn had dropped him.

Resuming our march at sunrise, we travelled twelve miles, the country assuming a slightly more rolling character as we advanced. We crossed many broad and well-beaten Indian trails, all going to the southwest and northeast, but none towards the direction we were travelling. Our guide, however, who had been full of confidence before, still retained his confident air, and assured me there was no doubt of our finding water a short distance beyond.

A half mile further, and he came back to tell that the distant mountain, towards which our course was directed, was not the one he thought, and that he was completely lost. I ought to have killed him there, but I did not.

We were thirty-two miles from water and in a country entirely unknown. Encamping at once, I despatched the two dromedaries to the east, while, with a few men on our strongest horses, I started to the west. On our line we travelled through some low hills, and following an Indian trail came suddenly upon a most wonderful sight. This was a chasm in the earth, or apparently a split in the very centre of a range of hills, from the top to the bottom.

Seeing that Indians had descended, I determined to try it, so, picking out the least precipitous part and scrambling down and leading our horses and zigzagging, we at last reached the bottom. Indian sign was abundant in the caves on either side, and a trail led up the middle of the ravine.

From appearances I should judge they wintered here, after gathering the piñon on the surrounding mountain sides. Exploring the cañon upwards for five or six miles, we found it ran out, so we ascended a steep hill, and, finding no water or any appearance of any, we turned our faces towards home. Arriving at camp, I found the dromedary men had found a river (the Little Colorado, I presume) about sixteen or twenty miles off, but very rough to approach. Our animals were now beginning to suffer very much, having been almost constantly at work for thirty-six hours without water; and one of the most painful sights I ever witnessed was a group of them standing over a small barrel of water and trying to drink from the bung hole, and seemingly frantic with distress and eagerness to get at it. The camels appeared to view this proceeding with great contempt, and kept quietly browsing on the grass and bushes. Unfortunately, the dromedary men had not gone down to the river, so that it was not certain that water, even though existing, could be got at, for these rivers, in going through cañons, are frequently inaccessible, so that, all things considered, it was safer to return, while the animals had strength to do so, to the water we had left, and start again, without guides, for, up to this time, they have proved a perfect curse to the party. Hitching up the teams, we commenced our retreat at dark. At about 3 o'clock in the morning it was found necessary to turn the animals out and drive them to water.

The moment they were released they started off in a gallop, (for they well remembered the last water we had left,) which did not cease, with many of them, until they arrived at King's creek. I arrived, with Thorburn, at 7 in the morning. This evening the animals will be sent back to bring on the wagons, and will probably be here by daylight. The weather is warm.

A heavy growth of pine and cedar covered the hills in every direction, around the great cañon I have mentioned, and extended as far as we could see from the high hill we ascended. The grass was dry gramma, which did not appear to have sprouted at all this year.

The camels were sent on in advance, and shortly after our arrival here, although, like the rest of us, they had been on the road all night, they were started back with eight or ten barrels of water for the camp at the wagons. Six of them are worth half the mules we have, although we have good ones.

September 20—*Camp* 18.—To-day the wagons arrived, the mules having been sent back for them last night. Every one looks wretchedly jaded, and all hands are glad to get back to King's creek again, and most of them a little sick of exploring parties.

It must be borne in mind by those interested in the road that this has been only a lateral exploration, and not the line of the road itself.

I am now getting ready, with five or ten men, to start in advance to explore the country, before moving on with the camp.

September 21—*Camp* 18.—Left, with Thorburn and ten men, at 4 in the evening, taking with us six breakers, of fifteen gallons each, of water, packed on camels, for the use of the mules and men. I took with me also, on this exploration, for the convenience of packing blankets and provisions, the small instrument wagon. At about 8 we encamped, after travelling across the plain, in a westerly direction, some ten miles, where the grass was good and wood abundant. At daylight we were off, still holding the same course, in order to turn the northern point of the long mesas I have mentioned as running out into the plain. Taking with me two men, I started more to the southward, into the mountains, and climbing the steep and rocky sides of the mesas we found ourselves, on gaining the summit, in a region of rough high table land covered with lava rock, but still very pleasing to the eye, for the timber was abundant—pine and cedar—and the grass a rich green and luxuriant. Through this beautiful country, abounding with deer and antelope, we searched ineffectually the whole day for water. To me the presence of game was conclusive evidence of the existence of water, and yet although we hunted faithfully, and were all experienced men, we had no success, and not a single spring could be found. At night we returned to the instrument wagon, which had followed a back bone, and by a more southerly course had reached the top of a high divide, which I determined to cross the next day in the prosecution of our search. Unfortunately the trails of the antelope and deer, which generally form good guides to the water hunter, in the rocky soil of the mesas, soon ran out, so that they were of no use. Birds too were abundant—jays, hawks, ravens, sparrows, and towards evening a flock of partridges gave us encouragement for a further search in the morning—nevertheless it was thought prudent to send back the instrument wagon to camp, as it would reduce the number of animals requiring water, and also men. At daybreak it was on its return, a dromedary having been started to camp to send out to its assistance water and fresh mules. Last night we watered our animals after their hard days' work, a fourth of a bucket each, and, as the day had been hot, it was only enough to tantalize them.

Starting at daybreak, we resumed our search, and passing through a great deal of pretty country, we came upon a ravine, at least what seemed one at the commencement, but which, on further examination proved a level and beautiful pass through a range of sand-stone mountains. The prospect was tempting, although it evidently led us far from home, and our animals, if no better success attended us, were sure to die under us for the want of water, leaving our own chance of life to depend on our getting back over a rough country, some fifty or sixty miles afoot. However, trusting to luck I determined to try it. Following down the pass, which I called after Tucker, one of my men, and a very worthy one, we found it to descend rapidly, but with a very smooth surface to the mouth, a distance of perhaps six miles. The width would not average over a hundred and fifty yards, and the direction was southwest. It seemed to cleave the mountain, which was of a bright whetstone character from summit to base, and opened into a wide valley of some twenty-five miles in length and ten in breadth, covered with grass so green that it seemed we must find water in it. Turning to the left, and going to the southeast at the base of the Sierra, which was a line of perfectly perpendicular rock for its entire length, we journeyed on for eight or ten weary miles to where the mountains, forming the southern boundary of the valley, united with the Sierra we had passed through. Here we found an easy path, and going through it and turning to the northward, we encamped at night on the dry bed of a stream, having travelled nearly fifty miles. The day was hot and dusty, and during this time we had watered our animals *once* with about four quarts each, and their distress was painful to witness. It was evident something must be done speedily, or we should loose every animal we had, and perhaps our own lives, for we knew nothing of the character of the country we had to traverse between us and camp, or whether, indeed, it was passable at all.

Camp was, by my estimate, sixty or seventy miles distant, bearing nearly north, and we had remaining one fifteen gallon keg of water for eight men and ten animals, which had already been exhausted for the want of it. Matters began to look squally. The camels alone seemed perfectly indifferent, and, like good fatalists, chewed their cuds in cheerful contentment. At day break we were on the road again, heading north towards camp, but having a terrible time of it over volcanic rocks and brush wood of cedar and scrub pine. We struggled manfully on until noon, when all the mules were completely done up, and it was evident they could go no further. I was fortunately riding a superb horse on the occasion, "Gray Eddy," full of strength and endurance, and I came to the conclusion to give him a bucket of water, and trust to his reaching camp with an order to send out immediate relief. He drank it eagerly, for his tongue was as dry as an old bone, and his lips parched and hot with fever. Exchanging my horse with Tucker for his broken down mule, I ordered him to proceed to camp at once, giving him his landmarks and bearings, and send us assistance, and in the meantime we would ascend a prominent point and keep up fires and smokes to guide the relief party to our camp. We had about a bucket of water remaining, and if Tucker got in at all, we could not expect him back for forty-eight hours. As for the poor animals, they hung around the empty water kegs braying huskily for what they were perishing for. Everything now rested on the gallant gray, and as if conscious of his responsibility the noble brute struck out boldly for the mountain which marked the direction of camp. Slowly we followed along to reach the point where our signal fires were to be kept burning. We had not gone over three miles when I observed a rugged looking cañon on the left, which seemed as though it might bear water. Dismounting, I climbed down the steep and slippery rocks to the bottom, and, after a short search, discovered small hole, under a projecting rock, containing water. Pursuing this discovery, I found, a hundred yards further down, a large pool of perhaps a thousand gallons. I fired my gun and pistols at once to halt the party which had passed on, and our famished animals being led down to the pool, plunged their heads to the eyes in cool water, and for the first time in three days, satisfied their thirst. May Stacey was started on his mule, now refreshed with water, at speed to overtake Tucker, which he succeeded in doing, the two returning to camp that evening. The mystery of so much game and so little water was now solved. Instead of looking for streams and rivulets, I found

I must look in the rocky cañon for pools and water holes. Acting on this, I found water next morning after a half hour's search, and in this region shall not fear for the future. The nature of the country beyond must determine the method of search when we get there.

Leaving the lucky cañon, which I called Alexander's, from one of the men who were with me, the next morning, we followed valley after valley, one opening into the other, until we reached the plain where I halted, and, watering our animals from the replenished kegs, made coffee and rested awhile, with the view of taking the moon for the next ten miles to camp. Starting sometime after dark with Thorburn, Tucker, and Davis, the remainder of the party being left to come on in the morning, we walked our animals over the plains, guided by the North star.

My horse walking more rapidly than the rest I gradually drew several miles ahead, and reached the rocky banks of King's creek at our camp about ten o'clock. Seeing the wagons quite close, and finding, as I thought, the camp fire where the mules were herded and no guard visible, I concluded they were all asleep, and that discipline had been relaxed in my absence. I determined to frighten them, so drawing my revolver, and giving two or three Indian yells, I fired it off. I hardly remember much that occurred after that. "Gray Eddy" wheeled at the first yell, and when I fired took the bit in his teeth and was soon rushing like lightning over the rough ravines and precipitous and rocky affluents which run in all directions from the plains into King's creek. My arms soon became as useless as if they belonged to somebody else a mile off, and, expecting to be dashed to pieces every moment, I was carried by the frightened animal many miles. Once I stopped him, but it was only for a moment, when he made a fresh start worse than ever, until at last, with a tremendous crash that made me see stars, we came down together. Fortunately his feet became entangled in the bridle and I was able to recover him, which was more than I could do for myself, for I remained sick and bruised on the ground until nearly morning.

In the meantime camp was all in confusion. The Indian yells had started every man to his feet, and for a while a regular stampede was the result of my experiment. To make the matter more mortifying, when I got back I found that the fire I thought was the guard fire was an old one left burning, and that the guard and mules had been removed a half hour before to another point some fifty yards off.

My admiration for the camels increases daily with my experience of them. The harder the test they are put to the more fully they seem to justify all that can be said of them. They pack water for others four days under a hot sun and never get a drop; they pack heavy burdens of corn and oats for months and never get a grain; and on the bitter greasewood and other worthless shrubs not only subsist but keep fat; withal, they are so perfectly docile and so admirably contented with whatever fate befalls them. No one could do justice to their merits or value in expeditions of this kind, and I look forward to the day when every mail route across the continent will be conducted and worked altogether with this economical and noble brute.

In the morning I shall send off Mr. Thorburn and ten men ahead, to Bill Williams' river, to explore for a road, and shall start myself with three to look for water in the intermediate distance. I am determined, before leaving, to make sure work, and know every foot of country between here and the Colorado, so as to make no mistakes. Our explorations to north and west, which we have carried on for the past two weeks, convince me that in that direction water is too scarce for a road, but I do not regret the trouble we have had in examining the country. The knowledge we have gained of it fully compensating for the hardships. The country we have been exploring to the north of our road is evidently that described by Captain Sitgreaves.

September 27—*Camp* 18.—The day has been passed in getting off Thorburn's expedition, which started at noon, and also that of part of my escort, which I determided to send back from this place, having no further use for them, and not wishing to deprive the quartermaster's department of the teams used for their transportation. I sent back a corporal and twelve men, with four wagons and their teamsters, retaining a sergeant and six men, with one wagon.

In the evening we repacked our wagons, ready for a start to-morrow, intending to move to Alexander's cañon, where we found water day before yesterday.

The weather is clear and pleasant, though cool at night. A few nights ago, ice formed in the bottom of a bucket.

The climate here is so pure and dry that we frequently dry mutton, when we have killed more than the rations, and keep it, without its spoiling, for a week. It is not found necessary to jerk it, but simply to lay it in the sun and air (sides and hams) on the bushes.

September 28—*Camp* 19.—We left King's creek at 3 o'clock, and travelled nine miles and a half, when we encamped on a slight eminence covered with excellent grass, and with a scanty growth of cedars; but where there was no water.

We passed over a rolling prairie, from King's creek to this place, having no timber upon it, but grass everywhere good. We saw many antelopes on the plain, the soil of which is clay mixed with gravel.

The weather this evening is quite cool, with a light southerly breeze and a few clouds. We arrived in camp at 6.

September 29—*Camp* 20—Left camp at 5.30 a. m., and arrived here, at Alexander's cañon, at 12.

Our road this morning was by the trail we made three days ago in going from this place to King's creek. We followed a gradually ascending valley the entire distance, from last night's camp, until within three miles of this, when we crossed a divide which intervenes between the waters flowing north into the great plain and those flowing southwardly into some of the tributaries of the Gila or Colorado. On either side of the narrow valley we came up stretched the mesas, which I have previously spoken of as running like headlands out into the plain.

Their slopes and broad flat summits were covered with pine and cedar, though the latter growth predominated. The grass, gramma, abundant on all sides.

The soil in places is rocky with a great deal of obsidian scattered over it; where it was not rocky, it was of clay and coarse gravel.

The weather to-day has been delightfully pleasant, reminding one of the pleasant autumn weather of Virginia or Maryland, though the nights are cold and the early morning air keen and fresh ; so that our mules made nothing of the fifteen and a half miles which we have travelled to-day.

On arriving here my first care was the pool of water we had left. On examination I found it but little diminished by evaporation, there being still enough left, I hope, for our purposes until we find more in advance of us ; though the delay of hunting ahead is very great, besides giving both men and animals much additional labor. If it were not that the grass is so good and abundant, our mules and horses would soon sink under this double duty ; but as it is, they are in fine condition ; thanks to the good grazing. We have made a southwest course to-day, and, to-morrow, hope to strike out more to the westward. Abundance of deer and antelope, constantly in sight, render our ride, this morning, a most agreeable one. The deer were of the species known as black-tailed. Bear sign was also frequent, though Cuffee did not show himself in person.

September 30—*Camp* 20.—To-day has been spent in exploring the country ahead for water. A fine pool and two springs were found, nine miles off, due west of us, and to this I shall move with the train in the morning.

Our present camp, at Alexander's cañon, is at the northern base of a high conical mountain, which we at first thought to be the Picacho of Whipple ; but it does not agree with his description or position. It is the southern termination of a long range of table mountains, dividing the waters flowing north into the Colorado and Little Colorado and those which find their way into the same river below the bend. The centre peak is sharp, and has upon its northern side a singular grove of aspen, growing on the steep ascent, near the top. Looking at it from the north, it has upon the right two smaller and lower peaks, and on the left, one ; altogether, with mountains Thorburn and San Francisco, it forms the most prominent land mark in this vicinity. The cedar growth here is quite heavy and abundant ; I measured one tree to-day sixteen feet in circumference, and it was by no means the largest I saw. Pine is scarce and small, though we occasionally find it in patches on the elevated mesas we are now encamped on. Yesterday, in exploring, I found walnut trees of small size, in many places. Within a mile of camp, I found a circular hole on the level table land, which much resembled Jacob's well, heretofore described, excepting that the sides were of volcanic rock. The soil over which my explorations led me to-day was generally of a rich character, producing everywhere fine grass ; for the most part it was clay and gravel, with occasionally spaces of considerable extent covered with large and loose volcanic rock ; timber everywhere. The weather is warm ; evening cloudy.

October 1—*Camp* 21.—At daybreak we were off, and travelling nine and a half miles west found an excellent camp at the water holes and springs discovered yesterday.

The centre peak of the mountain, spoken of yesterday, bears from our camp east by south.

From Alexander's cañon the road ascended almost imperceptibly to the table land, and descended from the divide almost as gradually. The country and soil is the same as that yesterday described. Several small conical hills are within sight a mile or two to the southward, and directly to the west a large bald hill or mountain, with steep sides, rounded top, and but little timber on it.

The morning was cold but the day has been warm and cloudy, so that we are in hopes of rain.

Our present camp is an excellent one; grass, wood, and water in abundance.

To-day is that fixed for the return of Thorburn's party, and we are looking for it with great anxiety, as we are all getting tired of this slow and tedious work, and look to his report of the country ahead, with hope of being able to recommence our old style of travelling. Leaving Alexander's cañon at 6, we arrived here at 9.

A fine black-tailed doe was killed this evening.

October 2—*Camp* 22.—Thorburn not having returned, I moved on southwest twelve and a half miles to the mouth of the Pass, (which I have named Pass Dornin, after Captain Dornin, United States navy,) discovered a few days since, while we were reconnoitering ahead.

The morning was cloudy, with a few showers of rain, but only enough to wet our buckskins thoroughly, without doing any other good.

The first three or four miles of the road to-day was rough and stony, but the latter part excellent; the soil was sand and clay.

On arriving at camp, I ascended a mountain which forms one side of the entrance to the Pass. It was very steep and high; but on reaching the summit I was fully repaid by the extensive view it afforded.

I am now convinced we are near Lieutenant Whipple's trail, (probably within fifteen or twenty miles,) but all traces of it are so completely obliterated that it is impossible to follow him. I think we are now within twenty-five or thirty miles of his Aztec Pass, and a little to the northward and westward of that point.

From the summit of the mountain, as I looked down, almost directly under was the camp, which was at the mouth of the Pass. Then came the view westward. The pass opened into a wide valley, bounded on the north by a high and precipitous mesas, and on the south by a long range of low mountains, apparently very rugged and broken. The valley itself was level and broad, being six miles at its narrowest part in width, and filled with fine grass. To the westward this valley seemed to stretch out to the full extent of vision. About fifteen miles off, near the centre of it, was a high table land or mesa, apparently unconnected with any other range, and rising abruptly and squarely out of the plain. Far, very far, in the distance, were dim mountains, which may be the chain running parallel with the Colorado.

To the southward I could see, over the range bounding the valley, another range, or at least the tops of high mountains, showing a valley to exist between, by the difference in the shades of blue. Turning to the eastward, I could see, stretching off to the southeast, an extensive valley, which seemed to contain in its wide spreading arms, Bill Williams, San Francisco, Sitgreaves, Kendrick mountains, and a host of hills of lesser note. Into this valley one would think some noble river would enter, to add to the fertility of the soil, as well as to the beauty of the landscape; but I regret to say that only a few meagre streams, containing no running water at present, find their way from the mountains to it, although, doubtless, springs exist throughout these mountains.

Tne pass at the valley on which we are encamped is approached by so gradual an elevation, that, except on inspection, it seems almost like a continuation of the great valley just mentioned. Its course is northwest, and it seems to be the only road left us, unless we cross the ridge to the mountain valley, which I have mentioned being shown by the difference of shade to exist in that direction. This I will look at to-morrow, as I shall then start on another exploring expedition, if Thorburn should not return. The valley we encamped at the entrance of is the same into which Tucker's Pass, discovered a few days ago, enters, that pass coming in at right angles to the one we are on, about ten miles west of our present camp. Wood at this camp is abundant, both of cedar and pine, but there is no water. Grass good.

October 3—Camp 22.—We are still looking anxiously for the return of Thorburn, who has now been absent six days. To pass the time more agreeably than lying idly in camp, I started out with Davis and Tucker to explore to the westward. We started at 9 in the morning and returned at 9 at night, never having left the saddle for five minutes since the hour of our departure. Our course was nearly west, and I suppose we could not have travelled less than forty miles, going and returning. Contrary to my expectations, we found the country easy for either wagons or horseback travelling. The mountains were generally lower than I thought from looking at them yesterday, and the ranges all tended to the northwest, with pleasant and wide valleys, filled with excellent gramma grass, on which numerous herds of antelope and deer were grazing. Timber, of cedar and pine, was everywhere abundant. The weather was cool and clear. The soil fertile, and of gravel and clay principally. I saw, in many places, a small black locust tree, but scarcely larger than an ordinary rose bush. We crossed one hill which seemed to be entirely formed of quartz, such as is found to contain gold in California. Towards sundown we found a few rude huts, probably the spring or last winter camp of Indians. A metata, and a few other of their very limited supply of household furniture, had been left to await their return. At this point I thought we had reached a fork of Bill Williams' river, as we were evidently on the head of a ravine, which, some distance beyond, connected with another in a rough deep valley or cañon, and to the southward a range of black serrated mountains looked like those called by Lieutenant Whipple the Black mountains. I regretted not having time to explore further, but it was nearly sundown, and we had twenty-odd miles before us to camp, and had started without bringing with us any provisions; so turning our backs upon what seemed a very interesting country, we returned, to reach camp at 9 o'clock. Should Thorburn not re-

H. Ex. Doc. 124——5

turn by to-morrow, I shall make another exploration more to the southward.   The weather to-day has been cool and pleasant.

October 4—*Camp* 22.—About the time I was preparing for my contemplated exploration to the southeast, to my great delight Thorburn came in.   He had discovered a small stream some thirty-five miles distant from our present camp, and, by hard travelling, had explored over a hundred and fifty miles of the country lying west and southwest of King's creek in the seven days of his absence.

This, with the explorations made by us from Floyd's Peak, as I have named the mountain described near Alexander's cañon, leaves only a quadrant lying to our southeast unexplored, within a radius of forty or fifty miles from Floyd's Peak.

Preparations were immediately made for our departure to-morrow at 3 o'clock   At that time we shall leave here, and, travelling through Dornin's Pass and the level valley beyond until midnight, we will encamp until daybreak, and hope to reach the water by 3 in the evening of the next day.   Thence, we shall make another exploration, which will take us to the Colorado river.

The weather is mild, clear, and very agreeable.

October 5—*Camp* 22.—The day has been spent in rest and quiet. The wagons are prepared for our night march.   At dark we left camp, and, ascending a very slight elevation, which makes the entrance through Dornin's Pass, we came upon the wide plain or valley beyond.   This was so level that we travelled it until midnight without a single stoppage, when we encamped in good grass, though without other wood than greasewood bushes.

On the hills to our left was plenty of cedar and pine, but as they were a mile distant, I did not care to go to them, as the men had eaten before leaving our last camp, and required rest more than food.

The night was mild and pleasant—only cool, not cold.   The soil of the valley was clay and gravel, and the grass abundant, though young and short.

We made thirteen miles and three-quarters.

October 6—*Camp* 23.—At daybreak we were up and off again before sunrise.   Pursuing the same level valley on a course nearly west northwest, we came some ten miles, the hills on our left gradually diminishing until the range gave out in two small buttes of regular and graceful slopes.   Here we crossed a gentle divide, and changed our course to one almost west, in the direction of the water for which we were going, and, travelling five or six miles further, encamped on some limestone hills, near a pool of water in the rocks on the summit. As we passed down the large valley this morning, the range of mesa mountains on our right, which I have called the Aulick range, extended as far as we could see to the northward and westward.   In places the perpendicular face of the rock, which I should think full a thousand feet in height, was covered with crimson colored blotches and white spots intermixed, and presented a most singular appearance. The wide valley which we had traversed diagonally continued on, doubtless to a great distance northwest, at the foot of these cliffs, and as far as we could see, without diminution of its width.   Thorburn not having had time to look out a wagon road to the water, I encamped some four miles from it, and, the mules having drunk all the water in the pool, they were sent on to the stream this evening under the charge of Mr. Davis.

To the westward the country begins to assume a rougher appearance, so that I shall make another exploration in that direction to-morrow.

I sent Saeveda this evening to the water with the mules to show the way, and also to endeavor to come to speech with the Indians who have their little corn patch there. In the event of their running off, and of his having no opportunity to speak with them, I sent some calico and other presents to be left in their lodges, and the men had strict orders to touch neither corn nor melons, or to allow their animals to do any damage whatever to the place. Poor creatures! their time will come soon enough for extermination when the merits of this road are made known, and it becomes, as it most assuredly will, the thoroughfare to the Pacific.

The soil to-day has been clay and small gravel mixed; the grass (gramma) good, though as yet short.

The weather has been windy, but otherwise bright and pleasant. Wood is abundant—cedars and a little pine.

We left this morning at half-past 5, and arrived here at noon.

I rarely think of mentioning the camels now. It is so universally acknowledged in camp, even by those who were most opposed to them at first, that they are the salt of the party and the noblest brute alive, that to mention them at all would only be to repeat what I have so often said of them before. They have been used on every reconnoissance whilst the mules were resting, and having gone down the precipitous sides of rough volcanic mesas, which mules would not descend until the camels were first taken down as an example. With all this work they are perfectly content to eat anything, from the driest greasewood bush to a thorny prickly pear, and, what is better, keep fat on it.

October 7—*Camp* 23.—This morning started at 9 o'clock, and crossing a hill to the eastward about a mile from camp descended into a valley running off to the westward. Following this valley, which was nearly half a mile wide, I found it one of many, all of which seemed to drain their waters into one cañon. Here, as I expected, we found water. Two fine springs bursting out of the side of the cañon at the base of its perpendicular sides afforded quite a stream and pool of excellent water. Stripping our saddles and turning our animals loose to graze on the fine grass which abounded thereabouts, we remained near an hour, and then starting again we returned to camp, reaching it at 9 o'clock at night.

On our way back, old Saevedra's mule gave out, which obliged me to leave all of the party to take care of him, excepting Thorburn and Davis. This old wretch is a constant source of trouble to every one, and his entire and incredible ignorance of the country renders him totally unfit for any service. I keep him moving, however, on all occasions, by way of punishment for putting himself upon us as guide.

The valley we descended this morning has a slope to the water discovered, so gradual as to make it difficult to judge from the eye how

Jimson Weed (poison)

water would run in it. Where we first struck it, it is bounded on either side by high rough hills and rocky bluffs, which, after following it a few miles, soften into low hills well covered with grass, and on the left a considerable amount of cedar trees. Descending it some ten miles these hills recede, so that it becomes a broad valley of a mile or two in width, and, indeed, the hills become so low that the whole may be taken for a plain of many miles circumference. It seems a basin at the lower or western limit, in which the different valleys, having united their waters, break through a range of low mountains in the cañon where we found the springs. How far this cañon extends, or whether we can pass through it with our wagons, remains yet to be seen. I did not explore it further than the water which we found a mile from the head.

From the head of this cañon, the lowest point reached, from which a view of the ground passed over could be taken, the basin is bounded on all sides apparently by mountains, and is without any outlet, that I could discover, excepting the valley by which we entered, and the cañon which contains the spring.

Our journey of to-day has convinced us that the water Saevedra found, and to which Thorburn was sent, is not, as we supposed it might be, the head of Bill Williams' river, since the one runs south and the other north. It may probably be Gampia's creek.

The water discovered to-day, after running south for some distance, turns abruptly to the north, in which direction it finds its outlet into the Colorado.

On going to the springs this morning to water the mules our men found the fresh tracts of Indians, and that they had taken the presents left for them.

The general course of the valley followed to-day was west 30° south ; the soil clay.

There was little grass in the bottom, but abundance on the slopes of the hills. The weather is pleasant and clear.

October 8—*Camp* 24.—Raised camp at daybreak, and taking our wagons down the rough hill into the valley, we descended the level bottom rapidly towards the water. Where we descended the hill we found on the rocks many hieroglyphics cut by the Indian race who have doubtless once inhabited this region, but have long since passed away. Unhappily, we have no Champollion to decipher these histories of a past race, or much that is interesting in the story of the red man of past times might be brought to our knowledge. The country described yesterday leaves but little to say to-day. We saw at a dishtance te black serrated mountain mentioned a few days ago ; both yesterday and this morning it bore nearly southwest.

At the springs we found jimpson weed growing luxuriantly. It was pleasant to see even this well-known weed, so common at home, at this distance from everything like civilization.

The banks of the stream running through the cañon of the springs are lined with small willow, and other bushes requiring water, from which I conclude water may be found at all times near the surface.

The two springs are both strong heads of water, and gush out of the rocks in a most refreshing manner to a thirsty man.

The entire day's journey of twenty miles has been down the gentle descent of the valley to the springs, and as smooth as a table the whole distance. At the springs the cañon is only about two hundred yards in width, but, I presume, widens below. I have called it Engle's Pass, after Captain Engle of the United States navy.

The sides are palisaded at the summit, and in places they must be eight hundred feet in height.

Sufficient timber for fuel and cooking may be found on the banks of the stream, and good grass covers the bottom everywhere. A better place for wintering with stock could not be found, as the turns and winding of the cañon afford a shelter from any winds that blow. The soil is rich loam. The climate to-day has been pleasant, though this evening the clouds threaten rain.

Our course has been for the day about southwest. We were eight hours travelling time in making the twenty miles.

October 9—*Camp* 25.—It rained on us nearly all night, wetting our blankets, and making all things uncomfortable, and we crawled out, shivering in the cold morning air. We got off at 8.30 and pursued the course of the cañon, crossing frequently the little stream which turned and twisted in its narrow bed as if anxious to escape. The morning was one of great anxiety to me. We were in the cañon, which narrowed a short distance below the springs, and the walls became almost precipitous from the base to the summit. The course also began to take a more southerly direction, and what with the course and the doubt as to whether the cañon might not close in entirely so as to oblige us to go back, I passed a very anxious morning. A few miles below camp, however, the cañon widened. two or three miles more and its creek ran through a bottom of three-quarters of a mile, and cotton-woods (only two it is true) enlivened the view with their bright green leaves. Further view was shut out by a long point which came down into the valley. I was now well satisfied we could get out; but the course, and how far we would have to go before doing so, still remained to be settled So far the road down the cañon had been most excellent; no rocks, and the crossings of the stream all so easy as only to require working in one or two places. On our way down and near the long point mentioned, we followed an Indian track, and among the rocks found a good spring of fine clear water. Several others were found by the men on the sides of the cañon.

Passing the point, our doubts were all set at rest most satisfactorily. The stream turned abruptly to the westward, and in that direction a glorious view broke on us. For full sixty miles an immense plain extended to the west, only bounded by a distant range of mountains in that direction, through which we thought we could see such great depressions as to make a passage easy. This, we trust, is the Colorado range. Directly west is a huge mountain, which I called Mount Buchanan, and connected with it by a chain; the roughest we have seen is another which I called Mount Benton. Near this seems an overlapping of the mountain with the range which runs to the north-west, where a pass seems to be easy. Due northwest is a depression in the northwest range which apparently reaches the level of the plain. Altogether, the prospect is the finest we have had on the road. This great plain to the northwest must extend to the Colorado, for our distance from that river cannot now exceed by much the distance which we can see.

Much Indian sign is presented about our camp. A few hundred yards below is a rancheria, deserted, likely, by its people on our approach. It probably contained some thirty or forty savages.

The soil of the valley is excellent; principally of decomposed granite and loam. Grass is very fine.

The day has been threatening, but no rain has fallen. We found no water in the creek where we camped, and I think the descent is so rapid that we are much more likely to find it in pools a few miles below, where it reaches the level of the plain.

We came nearly ten miles to-day ; six on a southerly course, probably south southwest and four west. The fresh Indian sign induces me to believe water may be found quite near us in the morning, but we encamped too late this evening to look for it. There are bushes and small willows enough here for cooking and fuel, but it is all small stuff. The mountains have cedar on their sides.

October 10—*Camp* 26.—While awaiting in camp for the mules which this morning had been sent up the creek to water, our geologist came into camp, much excited, to inform me that while engaged in cracking stones on the mountain side, three Indians had crept up to his gun a short distance from him, and, after taking it, had drawn their bows upon him, and he was obliged to beat a rapid retreat to camp, which, fortunately, was not over half a mile from him. I immediately sent my three boys, May, Ham and Joe, to look after the thieves and to bring them into camp. They did not succeed in finding them, though they trailed them to the spot. Here they found shoe tracks an extraordinary distance apart, and of large size, coming directly towards camp; but as our geologist says he walked on his return, these could not have been his, especially as the toe had made deep impressions in the sand. We are at a loss, therefore, to know to what tribe they could belong, as shoes seem to be a luxury only indulged by the most civilized nations. On returning to camp the boys saw two Indians quite near, who immediately fired their arrows at them. This was returned by double-barrelled guns, and hearing this at camp, Mr. Thorburn and I started at once with our guns in the direction of the sound. A few hundred yards from camp, in the bottom of the valley, we saw the Indians running, and the boys hot foot after them, both parties firing as they ran. We immediately joined the chase, which proved very pretty practice for a while, but soon began to tell on the lungs. Some of the men having followed us, I directed them to return to the wagons and mount the horses and mules we had retained. This done, we all continued the chase. In a few minutes the mounted party joined us. I ordered the men by no means to kill the Indians, but to take them alive. Directly opposite camp is a dark red butte very rocky, high and steep. Here we fairly ran them to earth near the top. The first caught was a boy apparently fifteen years of age ; but where was the other ? We had completely surrounded the conical peak of the hill, and though a minute search had been made we had not found him. I was positive I had seen him while balancing myself upon a slippery rock, but in jumping off it I had lost him in an instant. Still I knew he was not over fifty steps from me; so putting Tucker at one point, and stationing others around, some were sent to the top, so as to form a complete cordon around the spot he had disappeared at. At last one of the men looking into a greasewood bush not larger than an ordinary rose bush, discovered him close to the root, lying apparently coiled around it, and so completely concealed that even within six feet of him he could not be seen. He was dragged from his concealment, roped and carried to camp. Here he was well fed and both of them clothed from head to foot, and they are now sitting quietly at the camp fire. I shall use them as guides to the Colorado, and then either take them on and bring them back next winter or allow them to return from that river.

We are now about sixty-five miles from the river. The weather is clear and pleasant.

This evening the boy appeared so young and unfit for a long journey, that I determined to release him and send him back to his people with all his fine clothes and presents.

We started with the wagons, and, after having gone three miles, encamped on the side of the mountain bounding the valley on the left. Wood is scarce, there being nothing but bushes, and the grass only tolerable.

In the morning the old Indian, our captive, has promised to show me a fine spring on the other side of the valley.

Our road this evening was about a west southwest course, and gravelly and stony in places. We crossed several small arroyos putting out from the mountain. The mountain on the left gives out within a mile of this place, and the wide valley we are in joins another equally wide, running to the southwest.

At dusk the boy was liberated and went off into the darkness rejoicing.

October 11—*Camp* 27.—This morning the good policy of setting the boy free has been made apparent. Shortly after daylight an Indian came in bringing the gun stolen from Mr. Williams the day before. I gave them presents—calico, blankets, handkerchiefs, &c., &c., half a sheep—and left them cooking their meat at our camp fire, in excellent humor with both themselves and us.

We started before sunrise, with our Indian captive as guide, and crossing the spur of the mountain, while the train passed around by the level valley, we found the spring in a narrow ravine high up in the mountain. It was a bold spring, and the tule or catstail growing on it proves it to be permanent water. I rejoined the train some three miles from the spring, and as the plain had been heavy, and the teams had made eight miles, I determined to camp where we met them, and send some men up with the mules and with picks and shovels to make a fine pool at the water. This done, I shall explore ahead again.

Grass (gramma) is pretty good at this place. Wood is indifferent, only bushes, and the soil loose clay, mixed with quartz and granite gravel. The weather is warm, clear, and pleasant. Last night there was a heavy dew. To-day I have seen a great deal of quartz, like the gold-bearing quartz of California. Some of the veins seemed very large, and were in positions to be easily worked.

The Indian fires were built all around us last night, but they made no attack upon us, nor did they attempt to stampede our mules. After taking a hurried dinner, I started with Thorburn, two or three of the men and my boys, under the guidance of the captive, to whom I promised liberty if he would show us water once more. We rode over the valley, or rather plain, for eleven miles, when we found a well some six feet deep, and apparently containing a sufficiency of water. It was nearly 10 o'clock when we returned—cold, hungry, and tired—to camp.

I determined to move camp to the well in the morning.

The grass here is pretty good, but no wood except bushes. The soil of the great valley we are in does not seem so rich as the general average of the land we have passed, and the grass appears to grow in large patches, leaving bare intermediate spaces.*

At the well, we found Indian signs, showing their presence around us ; but none came in sight.

October 12—*Camp* 28.—Starting at dawn we travelled by the easy plain over to the spring. Before leaving camp I started off old Saevedra to look for water, which, he says, he camped at somewhere about here fourteen years ago, but does not remember the exact spot. I sent with him Ham, May, and Joe, and the whole party under the charge of Tucker.

Our camp from the well, which I have called Butler's well, from one of my men, appears to be completely hemmed in by the most rugged mountains. The great valley is bounded on the north by the Buchanan and Benton ranges of mountains, and on the south by a rugged mountain I have named Harry Edwards' mountain. All the intermediate spaces are filled up with rough and ragged ranges of lower elevation. To the northward and eastward is a range of high, frowning, dark mesas, along the base of which and turning to the northward runs the dry stream, on which we encamped in Engle's Pass, (as I have called the cañon down which we came to the great valley;) and where we are to leave the valley is a problem yet to be solved, involving further exploration.

Fresh tracks of Indians at and around the well show them to be quite plentiful in our vicinity.

At 3 o'clock Tucker returned to inform me that Saevedra had found his spring, and that it was a fine running water. I was pleased to hear this on two accounts : In the first place, the supply in the well proved insufficient ; and in the next, it was the only thing old Saevedra had found, that he started to look for, since our departure from Albuquerque. Before he went out this morning, he told me that if he could only find this water the direction to three others would come directly back to his mind, and that they lay on a good course for us to the Colorado.

Leaving Butler's well, we journeyed six or seven miles over the

---

* I changed my opinion returning. We found the grass in this valley everywhere abundant.

great valley to the south, and encamped at the head of the cañon in which the spring and little stream rises. The grass is indifferent, and no other wood than bushes.

The road is excellent. The soil is loose and in places covered with volcanic pebbles and gravel.

October 13--Camp 29.--At an hour before daybreak the bugle sounded, and by light we were on the road.

At the head of the cañon we had about fifty steps of rocky road, which delayed us awhile, making it passable for the wagons. This over, we came rapidly down the level bottom of the cañon to the fine clear water of the spring, which we reached in five miles. This place—I refer to the cañon—differs in no particular from that already described as Engle's Pass. The character of the rock, the palisaded sides, are just the same. We found here plenty of wood for cooking ; but the grass is scarce at the spring, though a mile or two above it there is plenty. I have called the spring after Saevedra.

I have no doubt that this pass, like Engle's, will lead to another great valley, or a plain, over which we shall travel without trouble to the Colorado.

The stream from the spring, after running a short distance, sinks into the gravelly bottom of the bed of the stream. It affords abundance of water for any number of animals.

The weather has become warm this evening, recalling the summer weather of the Del Norte.

The mesquite growth also begins again to show itself, and other shrubs that grow in a warmer temperature than we have lately experienced in the more elevated region we have passed over.

Breakfast over, Mr. Thorburn, the boys, and myself started ahead to explore, leaving the wagons to follow on our trail. Emerging from the mouth of the pass, which I called the Boys' Pass, after May, Ham, and Joe, who were the first to enter it, we came upon a vast plain

Directly in front of us stretched a chain of high mountains cut into fantastic peaks and shapes of all kinds, and about fifteen miles from us.

To the northwest and southeast the view was unbounded, only two peaks appearing in the distance about the centre of the plain in the southeast　Directly ahead appeared in the centre of the mountain range a single peak, rising sharp and clear above the surrounding mountains ; and here the mountains seemed to form a pass, towards which we directed our steps. The plain appeared to be endless, and travelling towards the opposite mountain until night we were still at a distance from the base. The plain was barren of grass and bore only a growth of worthless bushes, but the ground was firm and strong and the travelling good. It was covered for the most part with fine gravel, and when beaten down will form an excellent road.

When night overtook us we unsaddled, and, tying up our mules, built a fire and cooked what little we had brought with us. Shortly after our fire was started, another at a long distance, perhaps eight or ten miles off, marked the position of our camp, and near to us, and between us and the mountains, we could see Indian fires. A guard of one man was kept on during the night, and we passed it pleasantly without disturbance from the Indians. In the morning as soon as it was light enough to see, we were off again.   Turning the point which makes out from the high peak, which I called Frank Murray's Peak, we entered a wide gorge, which seemed to cut the mountain far up towards its centre.   It was rough with stones, and overgrown in places with willow and rank weeds, through which Indian trails with fresh tracks and other signs, showing their immediate presence.   A few rude lodges, and a patch or two of pumpkins, were also found on the borders of the dry bed of the creek.   We found a fine bold spring about three miles from the entrance of the pass, and pursuing our way soon came to a short but steep hill at the end of the gorge, which seemed to be the summit of the pass.   Ascending this, the river lay below us.   We had arrived at the end of our long journey.   So far, without an accident.   Only those who have toiled so far, with life, reputation, everything staked upon the result, can imagine the feelings with which I looked down from the heights of this mountain upon the cotton-woods and shining surface of the river far below us.

At a great distance to the northwest, a snow-capped chain of mountains marked the Sierra Nevada, the mountains of my own State, and my heart warmed as I thought of the many friends beyond that distant chain who were looking anxiously for my arrival, and who would share with me the feelings of gratified pride with which the result of a successful expedition would be crowned.   Both the descent and ascent of the hill was sharp, and I therefore determined to pack the loads over on the camels, so as not to distress our mules.

Descending the hill we met the train coming up the pass, and having found another large spring below the first we encamped near it.   Here also was a patch of pumpkins and lodges.

In coming down the pass from the summit, I found Indian tracks over those made by our mules in going up, so that they had passed over our trail within an hour, and were doubtless hidden close to us in the bushes as we passed.   Poor creatures! if they had known me better, they would scarcely have hidden out of sight, or missed the blankets and shirts I would have given them had they come in.   The weather is warm.

In the evening we moved a mile further up the pass to the second spring, where we found, as at the first, a few acres of coarse bottom grass growing luxuriantly, and quite enough for one night's feed for our mules.   I sent the boys to the summit to make fires as signals to the Mohaves that we came as friends, and desired to trade.

It is about twelve or fifteen miles yet to the river, and from the Indians living there, who are a fine, large, bold race of agriculturists, we hope to obtain corn enough to feed our animals all the way from here to California.

I shall go into Fort Tejon to recruit and refit, as we have but ten days' provisions, at half rations, left, which short fare is owing to our having been misled by the miserable Leco, our guide.

October 15—*Camp.*—This morning we spent in unloading the wagons and packing the camels over the hill.   I sent Saevedra ahead with the boys to find a water to encamp at, between the summit and the river.   We might easily have avoided this mountain by going on the plain I have described as extending to the northwest, and turning the point of the mountain there where it gives out ; but my instructions direct me to a point opposite the mouth of the Mohave, and these waters make it easy for emigrants to make the drives, besides which the Mohaves, from whom breadstuffs, vegetables, such as beans, corn and pumpkins, may be obtained, do not live to the northward of this point, and which becomes important for these reasons.

We gained the summit without difficulty, and found it only a mile and a half from the spring.

Only a quarter of a mile was steep, and the whole was accomplished without double teaming.

The descent looked so steep that I determined to encamp on the top and make it in the morning. We had a slight shower of rain during the night.

October 16.—The whole morning has been employed in getting down the mountain, which, though not over three-quarters of a mile, was difficult to pass over, being steep and rocky.

Emigrants cannot pass here until the hill is worked. I estimate the expense of making this mountain pass a good one, and a good road for emigrants, at five thousand dollars.

In coming down the mountain, the little buggy used for the carriage of the instruments upset and broke a wheel, which is the first breakage we have had since leaving. As the chronometers had been taken out no harm was done, and as it had fulfilled the purpose for which it was purchased, and our journey was accomplished, I did not care to encamp to repair it, especially as the camels, with the tool chest, by a mistake of the gentleman having charge, had been carried many miles beyond the place I had intended for them ; thus, to our regret, separating our party a considerable distance, as they had with them all that remained of our rations.

October 17.—At daylight we were at work, and, passing down an arroyo making out of the mountains, encountered a short hill of not over fifty yards, which, on account of the arroyo running through a narrow chasm, we were forced to cross, in order to get back into the arroyo again lower down. The passage of this hill which we were obliged to work down cost us nearly all the morning. Once over this, we descended the dry bed of the arroyo rapidly. Here the Indians began to pour in upon us from the Mohave villages. First, two or three, and then by dozens. They were a fine-looking, comfortable, fat and merry set ; naked excepting a very small piece of cotton cloth around the waist, and, though barefooted, ran over the sharp rock and pebbles as easily as if shod with iron. We were soon surrounded on all sides by them. Some had learned a few words of English from trafficking with the military posts two hundred and fifty mile off, and one of them saluted me with : "God damn my soul eyes. How de do! How de do."

A few miles down the arroyo the growth of a patch of cottonwoods and willows announced the presence of springs ; but we did not wait to examine, though some of the party found water there. Shortly after we left the arroyo, and coming out on the left bank, followed an excellent Indian trail leading us directly to the river.

Night overtook us a mile before we reached the river. The plain over which we passed bore neither wood, water, nor grass, so that our camp was a rough one, and only enlivened by the Indians who brought some pumpkins, which we purchased, and baking them, we made an excellent supper.   Weather during the day has been warm, and the soil barren.

The distance made to-day has been about eight miles, on a course nearly west.

October 18.—This morning the mules were sent off before daybreak to water.   We had tried ineffectually to get them to the river last night, but found it impossible on account of the brush wood.

Camp is crowded with Indians again this morning, some bringing melons, others corn, and others beans, &c., to trade for old clothes, worn out shirts, handkerchiefs, or almost anything of ours they fancy. They are shrewder at a bargain, though, than our men, whose keen appetites cannot bear the delay necessary to a successful trade.   The watermelons, cantelopes, and pumpkins, are of excellent flavor and fair size.

In the river bottom, which is several miles wide, and of very rich soil, we found grass and wood in great abundance.   Trading with the Indians, in a day we had secured a hundred bushels of corn and beans, pumpkins, watermelons and cantelopes, to last us to the settlements. Here my journey, as far as the road is concerned, terminated.   My instructions directing me, in the event of a want of provisions, to proceed to Fort Tejon and procure them there.

Crossing my wagons over the river on the common air beds which I had brought for the purpose, and the use of which I recommend to others, I followed the United States surveyor's trail from the river to Los Angelos, my wagons and train taking the right hand road, and coming directly from the Mohave to the Fort Tejon.   Here I remained until about the 1st of January, when I commenced my winter journey homeward, arriving at the Colorado January 23, 1858.

Saturday, January 23, 1858.—We reached the Colorado river early in the morning, having encamped in a rain-storm the night previous a few miles from it.   Shortly after leaving camp, my clerk, F. E. Kerlin, who with two of my party had been despatched the day previous in order to have my boat ready for crossing, was seen returning. Various surmises were immediately started as to the cause, and as soon as he was within speaking distance he was questioned eagerly for the news.   He gave us a joyful surprise by the information that the steamer "General Jesup," Captain Johnson, was at the crossing waiting to convey us to the opposite side.   It is difficult to conceive the varied emotions with which this news was received.   Here, in a wild, almost unknown country, inhabited only by savages, the great river of the west, hitherto declared unnavigable, had, for the first time, borne upon its bosom that emblem of civilization, a steamer.   The enterprise of a private citizen had been rewarded by success, for the future was to lend its aid in the settlement of our vast western territory.   But alas! for the poor Indians living on its banks and rich meadow lands.   The rapid current which washes it shores will hardly pass more rapidly away.   The steam whistle of the "General Jesup" sounded the death knell of the river race.

Accompanying Captain Jchnson, was Lieutenant White, of the United States army, and fifteen soldiers as an escort, which, with as many rugged mountain men, and the steamer as a fort, made a dangerous party to meddle with.

In a few minutes after our arrival the steamer came alongside the bank, and our party was transported at once, with all our baggage, to the other side. We then swam the mules over, and bidding Captain Johnson good bye, he was soon steaming down the river towards Fort Guma, three hundred and fifty miles below. I confess I felt jealous of his achievement, and it is to be hoped the government will substantially reward the enterprising spirit which prompted a citizen, at his own risk and at great hazard, to undertake so perilous and uncertain an expedition.

I had brought the camels with me, and as they stood on the bank, surrounded by hundreds of wild unclad savages, and mixed with these the dragoons of my escort and the steamer slowly revolving her wheels preparatory to a start, it was a curious and interesting picture.

The camels, immediately on my arrival, for the sake of testing their capability of withstanding cold, I had placed in camp within a few hundred yards of the summit of the Sierra Nevada, and to this date they have lived in two or three feet of snow, fattening and thriving wonderfully all the while. Lately, in a terrible-snowstorm, the wagon, carrying provisions to the camp, could proceed no further. The camels were immediately sent to the rescue, and brought the load through the snow and ice to camp, though the six strong mules of the team were unable to extricate the empty wagon.

At the river I bade farewell to Major Blake and the officers who had accompanied me, and the same evening commenced my homeward journey. My object in undertaking a winter journey is to test the practicability of the road surveyed last summer for winter transit. For this purpose I have taken with me a party of twenty men, and hope to reach home in March.

We did not go far the first day, and shall not to-morrow, as I desire a day to regulate my party, and the mules cannot find very good grass for the first forty miles of the road. We encamped in a clump of willows, fifteen miles from the river.

January 24.—Started late and crossed the mountain to Murray's springs; the Indians of this side of the mountain, who are not friendly, yelling at us as we passed down the cañon, and showing themselves at a respectful distance on the high bluff on either side.

Grass tolerably good. Willow and mesquite wood plenty. Water is abundant, much more so than when we passed last summer. The weather cold.

January 25.—Breakfasted at 4 and off at 7. The night was passed without trouble from the Indians, though they shouted at us as we left camp from the hills where we saw their camp fires, which had been divided from ours by a small intervening ridge. The morning was cold and raw, and a keen easterly wind made walking much more agreeable that riding; accordingly, most of us walked for ten or fifteen miles towards Saevedra's spring. We passed close under Frank Murray's Peak, and, by going around the base, avoided a steep hill which we came over on the previous journey, and which is the only pull for a loaded wagon between Saevedra's spring and the summit of John Howell's Pass.

I am pleased to find how clearly our wagons have defined the road we explored last summer. The Indians have already commenced to follow our broad well beaten trail, and horse, mule, moccasin and bare-footed tracks are quite plenty on the road. At Saevedra's spring we found the greatest abundance of water, and our mules having drnuk, we filled our canteens and came on to the end of the "Boys' Pass," and encamped, having made twenty-five miles.

Grass abundant, and wood, though small, in quite sufficient quantities.

I ascended this evening the steep mesa or rocky bluff which forms the pass, and found an entensive table-land, stretching in every direction, and covered everywhere with excellent grass.

The latter part of the day pleasant, though the morning was cool. At noon the barometer was 50°.

January 26.—Up at 4 and left camp at 7. Coming out of the "Boys' Pass'," we left our wagon trail road, and striking a direct course down the broad and beautiful valley for our former day camp, we travelled until we entered the cañon of our first camp, from Hemphill spring. The valley we have travelled to-day is one of the most beautiful and extensive on the entire road. It is in extreme length not less than sixty miles, by a width of fifteen, and is filled with the most luxuriant grass in every part. As yet we have only discovered three waters in it, Via's spring, Butler's well, and a small spring at the head of it; but subsequent explorations will doubtless discover more, as there is evidently a number of Indians living in it. Although surrounded by high mountains—Buchanan, Benton, and Harry Edwards'—it is very easy of access and egress from the character of the passes. A large number of deer, antelope, and big horn tracks, show it to be well supplied with game, which, finding abundant grass, probably seek its warmth in winter, and retreat to the neighboring mountains during the heat of summer.

The grass is gramma.

It was my intention to have encamped to-day at the spring where we sent our horses to water from the Cosmino camp, but arriving in the night we were unable to discover the locality, and having passed Via's spring, Butler's well, and the little one, we were obliged to seek our blankets supperless; but our mules fared well, the grass being excellent, and the cañon smooth, level, and a mile wide.

Thermometer 48° at 8 p. m.

January 27.—Determined to lay by and shoe the mules. Up at 4 and found the spring a short distance from us. It is a beautiful one; the water pouring over the rock is received in a basin of some twenty feet diameter and eight or ten deep. Coming down the cañon it lies to the right hand, where a cañon coming in from the left widens the valley to a beautiful camp full of fine grass. The spring of the first water, on entering the cañon at its commencement, is three or four miles above. The weather clear and cool. Thermometer 50° at noon.

This morning, at 2 o'clock, we had a skirmish with the Indians. We lost one mule, killed with arrows, and another badly wounded.

At 2 o'clock thermometer 30°.

Two of the Indians who attacked us last night were slain this morning.

January 28.—Up at 4 and off at 6.30. Left Truxton's spring, travelled up the cañon by White Rock spring, and entered the wide valley leading to Hemphill's spring.

There is snow on the ground in patches which are rapidly passing away. Leaving our road at the head of the valley, we took a course nearly east, through some low hills covered with fine grass, and encamped among some cedars near the valley into which we entered by Dornin's Pass.

Gramma grass abundant.

Thermometer at sun down 45°.

A few Indian tracks seen to-day.

January 29.—Up at 4 o'clock and off at 6 30. The night pleasant. At midnight the thermometer was 36°, and at noon 76°. We rode all day in our shirt sleeves. Crossed some easy hills, through a fine forest of cedar and a little piñon pine. Grass everywhere abundant. By crossing the low hills we came directly east and entered the broad valley opposite Tucker's Pass, bearing straight for Dornin's Pass, and keeping along the foot of the hills which we passed some distance to our left as we were going over, and which form th boundary on that side of the valley into which both Dornin's and Tucker's Passes enter. We found some snow on the hills, but not enough to cover the ground, except where it had drifted. In the valley there was none. Encamped among the cedars at Dornin's Pass. Grass luxuriant and green. Saw a large band of antelope, and killed some rabbits. Indian tracks have been seen to-day, but old, probably a week.

Thermometer at sun-down 65°, at 8 p. m. 39°.

January 30.—Up at 2 and off at 3. The morning bright and clear. At daybreak the thermometer 31°. We found no snow on the road, and but very little at Worley's cañon or Smith's spring, where the water was abundant and grass excellent. Encamped in a grove of cedar trees, with which the country hereabouts is covered. Here I determined to pass the day, as we had yesterday a fatiguing march, and our mules want rest.

It is pleasant to see our old camps again, and to recall the anxious hours we passed at them when in doubt as to what we were to find ahead of us. At present we are under Floyd's Peak, which, for so long a time on our previous journey was our landmark in returning from our exploring expeditions, and its snow-capped summit looks as pleasant now as the face of an old friend.

At noon the sun was bright and warm, and the thermometer at 75°.

January 31.—Up at 4 and off at 6. Travelled directly east from Alexander's cañon, in which we found abundance of water, and left our road at that place and travelled in a straight line for San Francisco mountain, the snow-covered peak of which made an excellent guide. Our way to-day has been over a country of great beauty, and exceedingly rich in grass and cedar timber. The face of the country is undulating, and the landscape most pleasing to the eye. Passed large tracts of land, on which we found a red sandstone, apparently fit for building purposes without any further labor than selecting the size of the stone required. The surface is flat, smooth, and shiny, and enough of it to build a dozen towns without making any apparent diminution of its quantity. All day long we have found abundance of water in every little hollow. These streams and holes I do not suppose are permanent, but caused by recent rains and snows, spots and patches of the latter being still upon the ground.

Thermometer, at 4 a. m., 31°; at noon, 61°; at 3 p. m., 61°; at sundown, 50°.

Encamped in a cedar grove. Grass abnudant. Weaethr bright, clear, and cloudless.

February 1.—Up at 4 and off at 6. Passed a rolling country in a direct line for Mount Sitgreaves, and so heavily covered with cedar and piñon that our progress was constantly retarded by the trees. The hills and valleys are covered with bunch and gramma grass. Crossing some fine valleys, the only places we found free of a dense growth of cedar, we came at 2 upon a dim trail almost invisible, which, from the occasional marks of a wheel tire having scraped a rock, and a bush here and there crushed and broken, I took to be Whipple's. Following this a short distance, we came to a tank in the rocks, which I supposed was the Lava spring of Whipple. The grass being excellent, and water and wood plenty, I encamped here. The day has been warm and bright.

Thermometer at noon, 71°.

I determined this morning to come in a direct line to San Francisco, and therefore shall leave Breckenridge spring to our left. From an elevation we saw Mount Thorburn in the plain far below us, and the most prominent object in that quarter, in fact, on the whole road, with the exception of Floyd's Peak and San Francisco. We saw very many deer and antelope tracks. Snow only occasionally in small patches where sheltered by the cedars and pine.

After noon the travelling generally became laborious from the softness of the ground, so that we make but short day's journeys.

February 2.—Up at 4 and off at 6. After travelling a mile we came to a large tank in the rocky cañon, which, from the sign about it of camp fires, I knew to be Whipple's lava spring. From this point I determined to go south of Mount Sitgreaves, and by that means to Leroux's spring in a straight line. We passed over a fine country— rolling hills and timbered land—and found no snow until we reached the summit of the plateau at the greatest altitude over which we passed it last summer. Here, on the foot of the mountain, it had drifted for probably twelve inches in height. The travelling being laborious, I encamped near where we made our day camp, after leaving Leroux's springs, last summer. Shortly after leaving Lava spring, in which there was abundance of water, we came to New Year's spring, which was also full, and in a mile or two more entered the noble forest of San Francisco. The old mountain covered with snow, relieved by the dark green patches of pine, and the plain at its base, with its black forest of gigantic timber, presents a beautiful sight as the sun is setting this evening.

Thermometer at noon, 39°. At sundown under the shelter of the mountain, 46°.

Leaving the plain, which was covered with snow, we sought shelter under a spur of Sitgreaves' mountain for a camp and found a warm corner and plenty of grass and timber.

February 3.—Up at 4 and off at 7. Found the snow from a foot on the level to eighteen inches in drifts. Put all the men, excepting enough to drive the train, on foot ahead to break the road. The leader was changed every few hundred yards and came behind to the end of the line, nevertheless it was tedious work as the snow was just hard enough on top to break through at each step. This lasted for three miles, after which we had no trouble. After travelling all day through the beautiful forest of pine which covers the country, at four in the evening came to our old camp at Leroux's spring. At this pretty spring, which breaks out of the side of San Francisco mountain and runs four hundred yards into the valley, we found, as everywhere else, the southern exposure of the mountain entirely free of snow and covered with fine grass. Here we encamped for the night. At daybreak, thermometer, 29°; at noon, 36°; at sunset, 31°. A keen and cutting northwest wind all day, filling the air with fine snow, or what the Canadians call pondice.

February 4.—My birth-day.

Up at 4, but did not get off before 8, the animals having good grass and the previous day's journey having been a fatiguing one.

Directly after leaving Leroux's spring the snow commenced getting lighter, and broad bare patches to appear by the time we had reached San Francisco spring, which we passed but did not go to. It had become so light and so little of it that the travelling became easy. After coming twelve miles we encamped at our old noon camp, the grass being excellent; and, moreover, I knew I could not go further than Walnut creek the next day, or between there and the Little Colorado; there is no wood, which is very necessary to one's comfort these cold nights. Our camp is a beautiful one this evening; a clear space of three miles around and skirted with lofty pine trees. We amused ourselves, as we strolled through the pine forest this morning, in shooting squirrels, which are abundant here and of a very beautiful species. Their ears are tufted and very long, the back a beautiful rich brown with silver gray on the sides and white on the belly.

At 4 a. m., thermometer 20°; at noon, 48°; at 3 p. m., 57°.

The day has been calm, cloudless, and very pleasant.

February 5.—Up at 4 and off at 6.30. Still travelling through the forest we came at noon to Cosmino caves. The snow for the latter part of the morning scarce, and even in the drifts and patches where it did exist light and thin.

Encamped about a quarter of a mile below the caves, where we camped in travelling west last summer. If any one should ever follow our trail, it must be remembered that the water at this point is

H. Ex. Doc. 124——6

not that found at our wagon camp at the caves, although that is generally sufficient, but in an immense tank a quarter of a mile or so below. This singular tank in the rock is from eight to ten feet in depth, about twenty feet in width, and seventy feet in length at this time, and I presume is lower now than at any other season of the year. An excellent entrance for animals is found at its lower extremity. Cutting the ice, which was a foot thick on the surface, the sun only reaching it at noon for a moment or two, our animals drank plentifully, and after eating dinner we again started on our journey. The grass here is the best gramma and very abundant. Timber in the greatest abundance ; cedar, pine, and piñon. The day very warm, calm, and clear. Indian horse and foot tracks seen on the trail all day and last night near camp. Entirely out of the snow, it being only visible on the distant hill tops.

Thermometer at midnght, 18° ; at 4 a. m., 18° ; at noon, 67° ; at midnight 22°.

February 6.—Up at 3 and off at 4.30 a. m. Shortly after sunrise came to Walnut creek, where we stopped for breakfast. Water not so plentiful as when we passed here outward bound. The grass very fine ; no snow at all. The morning calm, clear, and cold. Walked from camp to Walnut creek. After breakfasting I determined to remain all day, as we found more water than we at first thought ; more than sufficient for all our animals and camp purposes.

Examined the ancient ruins near here. We found one house in which the floor had been laid in adobe. The ground was covered for many acres with pottery, and some fine arrow heads were found near the ruins. Looking more closely we discovered that what we at first took for piles of loose stones and earth were the ruins of houses, in one of which we could trace five distinct rooms separated by what remained of the partition walls. Behind one of these the ground on stamping gave forth a hollow sound ; but having no pickaxe with us, we could not investigate the cause.

Thermometer at 4 a. m., 27° ; at noon, 70° ; at sundown, 37°.

February 7.—Up at 4 and off at 5 a. m. We came to the Little Colorado at noon, and encamped a few miles above our old camp. We found the river very much lower than when we passed in September, though from the ground it was evident much rain had fallen lately.

The weather is warm and pleasant though a good breeze is blowing from the westward.

Thermometer at 4 a. m., 33° ; at noon, 67°.

February 8.—Up at 4 and off at 5 a. m. Soon after starting we left the river and followed our old cut off, and passing the holes where we watered last fall, and which we found equally full to-day, we came soon after to the little stream which we found running when we passed it the first time. Here we found abundance of water, but not running as formerly. Crossing the playa, through which the water runs off, and leaving the road to our right hand, we entered a small cañon in which we found plenty of grass, shelter from the wind, and a considerable quantity of brush-wood, where we encamped.

The day has been rather disagreeable, and a stiff breeze (double reefed topsail) blowing in our faces, with an overcast sky, has made it the most uncomfortable day we have had on the road.

Thermometer at 4 a. m., 25°; at noon, 58°; at sundown, 45°.

February 9.—Up at 4 and off at 6. After leaving camp a short distance we came upon a fresh trail of Indians, which we followed as far as Davis' creek—thirteen miles. Here I crossed the river. Davis' creek is much fuller than when we passed, and the river is rising.

Last night the wind blew half a gale, and though the morning was calm it is now blowing fresher than ever. Fortunately we have abundance of timber, and the cotton wood on the river makes a good lee for us.

Found some fine ducks in ponds near the river, of which I killed two.

Thermometer at 4 a. m., 31°; at noon, 58°; at sundown, 45°.

February 10.—Up at 4 and off at 7 a. m. Travelling up the river, and passing two of our old camps, we encamped near Cottonwood Fork, in sight of Mount Whipple, San Francisco mountain being hull down to the westward. Found a good camp, where some cedars and cottonwoods grow, near the river bank. The day has been cloudy, with rain this evening and a prospect of it all night long. Passed two old Indian trails—nothing fresh.

Thermometer at noon, 31°; at sundown, 45°.

February 11.—Up at 5 and off at 7.30. It rained on us all night in drizzling showers, as well as some little this morning. The day raw and squally, with heavy clouds.

After travelling eight miles we left the river at the mouth of the Puerco. The more I see of the Little Colorado the better I like it. The stream is of the size of the Gila, but to be likened to that fresh water abomination in nothing else. The soil seems fertile and bears good meadow grass in all parts, while the plains, extending from its banks as far as one can see, are covered with rich gramma grass. The growth of timber in the bottom is in places very heavy and almost entirely cottonwood, but on the left bank, a mile or two from the river, cedar is abundant along the whole length of the stream. All who are with me, and who have been raised in the south, declare it to be excellent tobacco and cotton land. I am not sufficiently acquainted with the culture of these products to give an opinion, but for stock of all kinds I should say that a better country is not within the United States. We found Cottonwood Fork running a brisk but muddy stream, and also the Puerco. Travelling up the latter river we encamped, a mile from our old camp, in abundant and excellent gramma and bunch grass at a half mile distance from the river. The little lagoons between this and the mouth were filled with water.

Thermometer at midnight, 28°; at 4 a. m., 32°; at noon, 54°; at sundown, 45°.

In the evening strolled with Joe Bell over the hills, and found the remains of a house. At another point overlooking the river found quite a number of ruins; apparently all the wood used had become petrified; as usual, a large amount of broken pottery ware, painted in various shapes, was laying around.

February 12.—It rained and snowed on us most of the night. This morning, shaking the snow from our blankets, we pursued our road at 8 o'clock, over the rolling plain, between the Puerco and the Xara. The snow passed off so rapidly, that by noon there was scarcely a trace of it to be seen, but the ground became so muddy that it made the travelling of to-day the hardest on our animals we have experienced during the voyage. At 2 o'clock we encamped on the Xara, having found a good lee under the cliffs, which bound the stream, and excellent grass and shelter for the animals. Our camp is about a mile below our former one, where we moored as we were going over. Weather squally, with rain, and occasionally spitting snow; wind blowing a gale from the northwest. Found the Xara twenty or thirty yards wide, and about two feet deep.

Thermometer at 5 a. m., 28°; at noon, 45°; at sundown, 42°.

February 13.—Up at 4 and off at 7 a. m. Found the stream we had encamped on was not the Xara; crossed the divide, and struck our old trail, where it comes into the Xara, and at 2 o'clock encamped on the Carisso, at our old camp. The travelling very heavy from late rains; found nothing but mud to put our blankets on, but rendered it comfortable by putting down a layer of bushes first. The stream running, and grass good and abundant.

Thermometer at midnight, 31°; at 4 a. m., 28°; at noon, 55°; at sundown, 48°.

February 14 —Up at 4 and off at 6 a. m. Travelled towards Navajoe spring; found some Indian horses, which we at first thought were strays or lost, we captured them at the Little Cotton Wood creek, half-way to the spring. In the evening, as we approached the spring, we found that many Indians were about, and not knowing whether they were Garroteros or Navajoes, we prepared for war. Just before arriving at the spring, discoverd a band of sheep, and from the Indians in charge heard that the large number of savages in the vicinity were Navajoes; watered our animals at the spring, and encamped a couple of miles from it in splendid grass, bunch and gramma. Cedar in abundance all over this country.

February 15.—Up at 5 and off at 8 a. m. The Navajoes were in camp early, but unwilling to trade horses. We left them with the promise that they would come over to Jacob's well and trade, we promising to wait until evening for them. Jacob's well I have previously described. It is the greatest curiosity of the kind I have ever seen. A third of a mile in circumference, a hundred yards in depth, and at the bottom a pool of water about thirty yards across, and fringed with cedar trees, rushes, and willows. It is descended by a spiral trail leading down the sides, which are of soft, yellow clay. Thermometer at 4 a. m., 25°; at noon, 75°.

February 16.—Up at 4 and off at 7 a. m. Met two Indians on the road, whom we supposed to be Garroteros. At noon came in sight of Zuñi, and encamped near the town.

Thermometer at midnight, 38°; at 4 a. m., 25°; at noon, 58°.

February 17.—Up at 4 and off at 5 a. m. Passing the Pueblo of Zuñi, we went a few miles beyond and encamped. Here I bought corn, of which these Indians have plenty, for our mules. They were all in great trouble, the Navajoes having stolen one hundred and fifty of their horses.

Here I parted with Sergeant Armstrong and the soldiers who had been with me so long. They were all excellent men, and I parted with them with great regret. I sent them back from this place to Fort Defiance, having hired of the Indians burros for their transportation.

Thermometer at midnight, 39°; at 4 a. m., 27°; at noon, 52°.

February 18.—Up at 4 and off at 5.30. Travelled by a very pretty valley to Ojo Pescada, which is one of the finest springs we have seen, and the land exceedingly fertile. The valley is reached by the trail from Zuñi, so gradually ascending as to seem a level road to the eye, though the elevation attained is considerable. The spring bursts a lively brook from under the rocks, and runs a bold stream at this season beyond Zuñi. Here the fine wheat of the Zuñians is principally raised, and the stubble remaining on the imperfectly cultivated patches, show clearly the natural resources of this beautiful valley.

Timber of both pine and cedar is abundant, and everywhere the richest grass covers the ground.

In the evening we came on by a beautiful, undulating country to the night camp, which we made in some cedars. The day has been warm and delightful, and the evening mild and clear.

There is a fine valley with a bold stream of water running through it, which may be reached by going three miles to the westward, across the mesa, at the Ojo Pescada. This whole country, with the exception of the valleys, which are clear and open, is covered with a dense growth of timber—cedar and pine.

Thermometer at 4 a. m., 26°; at noon, 60°.

February 19.—Up at 3 and off at 5 a. m. One would have to deal in superlatives altogether to describe the beauty of the country through which we have passed this morning. When at 9 a. m. we reached Inscription rock, I was tired of exclaiming, as every hundred yards opened some new valley, "how beautiful." The rock itself seems to be a centre from which radiates valleys in all directions, and of marvellous beauty. It rises grandly from the valley, and the tall pines growing at its base give out long before they reach the top of its precipitous face. Inscriptions, names, and hieroglyphics cover the base, and among the names are those of the adventurous and brave Spaniards who first penetrated and explored this country, with dates as far back as 1620. The race has long ago passed away, and left no representative of Spanish blood behind them. Those with us looked with listless indifference at the names of the great men of their nation, and who had made it famous centuries ago, cut by themselves upon this rock, and turned off to take charge of the mules, which is about all even the best of them are fit for.

The rock is some three or four hundred feet in height, and the spring almost hidden in the cavity of it; the face is perpendicular. The valley is ten miles in width, rolling but not hilly, and dotted over with clumps of pine and groves of cedar. A thick forest of pine covers the mountain, which defines the limits of the valley.

In the same valley with "Inscription rock" (as the name has been changed from the pretty old Spanish one of "El Moro") are, as I am informed by a Mexican of my party well acquainted with the country, four fine waters. The first, a large tank called El ojo del Trinidad, bears north northeast from this spring, and is two leagues distant. The next is the rivulet of the Muertas, (so called because of some people having been killed by the Indians,) bearing north northwest, or northwest, and ten miles distant. The next, the rivulet of La Savoya, bearing northwest by north, or west northwest, and twelve miles distant. The fourth is Los Nutinas, which is the largest, and bears west by north, and is fourteen miles distant.

On the summit of the rocks are ancient ruins, the walls of which are four feet in thickness. They are square, one hundred and seventeen yards in front. To the west the mouth of a natural inclosure opens into the heart of the rock, containing within its walls from twenty to thirty acres of level land, and growing in it the finest pine timber. The sides are from one to two hundred feet in height. The ground is covered with fine grass, and the whole may be closed by a wall or fence of thirty-five or forty yards length. Leaving this beautiful place with regret, we travelled up the valley some miles further, through a country of the same character, and encamped for the night.

Thermometer at 4 a. m., 28°; at noon, 70°; at sundown, 32°.

February 20.—Up at 4 and off at 5 a. m. All the morning passing through a fine open forest of tall pine, with extensive open glades and meadows at short distances. At noon we came to the beautiful valley of the Agua Frio. It is not very large, but is the finest we have yet stream issuing out of the head of it is clear and cold, but does not run seen. Its length is about five miles by one and a half in width. The over a mile before it sinks. The soil is exceedingly rich, and the hills bounding it covered with pine, and among the trees, which are not thick or scrubby, the finest grass. We had at this point crossed the Rocky mountains, but our passage had been through a country of such beauty that we could scarcely recognize, in the fairy land we had been travelling in, these rugged barriers, as they have been considered, to our westward progress in civilization. The temperature of the weather at the summit was delightful. The sun clear and bright. The trees green and luxuriant, and nothing but here and there a patch of snow reminded us that the winter was not yet passed.

Descending gradually by a most pleasant trail through beautiful valleys, and without crossing a hill, we came to our night camp, in a fine grove, where we found a fine pool of water and abundance of grass. As for the latter, that may be found everywhere. In the evening a stiff breeze blew up from the westward. It was a free wind, however, and we bowled off before it handsomely. Thermometer at 4 a. m., 30°; at noon, 50°; at sundown, 30°.

For a better description of the country through which we have been passing for the last three days, I refer to the very interesting report of Captain Simpson, United States army.

February 21.—Up at 4 and off at 5 a. m. Still descending gradually over a fine country we came to the Gallo. Crossed many streams of lava, which appear to have rolled in a fiery torrent just as a mountain stream from the hills. Crossing the rough face of this, we encamped at 10 near our old place on the Fort Defiance road, having been absent seven months. Here my labors ended; the main road to Fort

Lefiance being intersected at this point by that which I have explored and surveyed to Fort Tejon, California.

Thermometer at 4 a. m., 35°; at noon, 77°.

A year in the wilderness ended! During this time I have conducted my party from the Gulf of Mexico to the shores of the Pacific Ocean, and back again to the eastern terminus of the road, through a country for a great part entirely unknown, and inhabited by hostile Indians, without the loss of a man. I have tested the value of the camels, marked a new road to the Pacific, and travelled 4,000 miles without an accident.

In the author's opinion no one did more to "tame the west" than Ned Beale, from his service in the Navy and becoming the hero of the Battle of San Pasqual, to crossing Mexico with a seven pound nugget to beat the Army to Congress with proof of the California gold discovery, to his adventures crossing the country 13 times on horseback, to managing a mule train transportation business in gold rush California, to serving as the Surveyor General of California, to serving as a Brig. General in the California Guard to help solve Indian uprisings in the state, to the camel expedition and building the first wagon road to California…Beale was truly unique. And that was only the first half of his incredible life and career. Along the way he put together four Spanish land grants at the south end of California's San Joaquin Valley. A 270,000 cattle and sheep operation now a public company that's added real estate development, wine grape vineyards, and oil fields to its success.

Beale went on to become the Minister to Austria Hungary, the most powerful coalition of countries at the time. There's so much more to the story of America's most unsung hero.

The author wishes to thank;
Carl Briggs and Clyde Francis Trudell for their excellent biography *Quarterdeck and Saddlehorn* from The Arthur R. Clark Company
And
Gerald Thompson for his excellent biography *Edward F. Beale & The American West* University of New Mexico Press

And

The Beale Library, Bakersfield, California

Books by L. J. Martin

L. J. Martin Collection

Westerns:
Against the 7th Flag
Blackjack Brannigan
Blood Mountain
Buckshot
Condor Canyon
El Lazo
Eye for Eye
McCreed's Law
McKeag's Mountain
Mojave Showdown
Mr. Pettigrew
Nemesis
O' Rourke's Revenge
Revenge of the Damned
Rugged Trails
Shadow of the Grizzly
Shadows of Nemesis
Stranahan
The Benicia Belle
The Devil's Bounty
Tin Angel (Western Romance Written With Kat Martin)
Two Thousand Grueling Miles
West of the War
Wolf Mountain

Historicals:
Rush to Destiny
Shadow of the Mast

Action-Adventure, Crime & Thrillers:
Bullet Blues
Crimson Hit
G5 Gee Whiz (The Repairman No. 2)

Judge Jury Desert Fury (The Repairman No. 5)
Manhunter Series
No Good Deed (The Repairman No. 4)
Overflow (The Repairman No. 8)
Quiet Ops
Target Shy and Sexy (The Repairman No. 6)
The Bakken (The Repairman No. 3)
The Blue Pearl (The Repairman No. 10)
The K Factor (The Repairman No. 9)
The Repairman (The Repairman No. 1)
Venom
Who's on Top (The Repairman No. 7)

Contemporary:
Blood Lines
Unchained
Windfall

Non-Fiction:
Against the Grain
California Cocina
Cooking Wild & Wonderful
Cornucopia: Building A Greenhouse
Killing Cancer
The Write Stuff
Write Compelling Fiction (with Craig Martell)

Anthologies:
Paul Bishop Presents: Tales of Murder & Mayhem
The American West
The Trading Post
The Traditional West
The Manhunter Series
Western Fiction 10 Pack
Wolfpack Publishing Western Boxed Set
The Clint Ryan Series

Short Stories & Short Story Collections:
Holy Hell
Second is the First Loser
Short Story Collection & More
Slopes of the Sierra
Small Crimes
To Ride a Tall Horse
Western Short Story Showcase

9 798597 555317